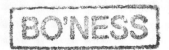

The best of
FRAGMENTS
FROM FRANCE

By Capt. Bruce Bairnsfather

Compiled and edited by
Tonie & Valmai Holt

All authors' royalties for this book will
go to the Charity, Help for Heroes

Pen & Sword
MILITARY

1st Edition published in Great Britain in 1978 by Phin Publishing
2nd Edition 1983 by Milestone Publications
3rd Edition 1998 by T & V Holt Associates

Published in this Format in 2009 by
Pen & Sword Military
An imprint of
Pen & Sword Books Ltd
47 Church Street
Barnsley
South Yorkshire
S70 2AS

Copyright © Tonie and Valmai Holt 1978, 1983, 1998, 2009

ISBN 978 1 84884 169 7

A CIP catalogue record for this book is
available from the British Library

Printed and bound in England
By CPI UK

Pen & Sword Books Ltd incorporates the Imprints of Pen & Sword Aviation,
Pen & Sword Family History, Pen & Sword Maritime, Pen & Sword Military,
Wharncliffe Local History, Pen & Sword Select, Pen & Sword Military Classics,
Leo Cooper, Remember When, Seaforth Publishing and Frontline Publishing

For a complete list of Pen & Sword titles please contact
PEN & SWORD BOOKS LIMITED
47 Church Street, Barnsley, South Yorkshire, S70 2AS, England
E-mail: enquiries@pen-and-sword.co.uk
Website: www.pen-and-sword.co.uk

FOREWORD

In early January 1916, the British weekly tabloid magazine The Bystander announced the imminent sale of its book 'Fragments from France' by Captain Bruce Bairnsfather, describing it as "48 pages of screaming comicality". By the end of the month, 'Fragments from France' appeared in bookstalls across England and was an instant hit. The book contained Bairnsfather's cartoons depicting life at the Front. The blob-nosed walrus moustached soldier 'Old Bill' caught the imagination and raised the morale of both the men on the front line as well as their families back home. Bairnsfather became a household name. He had eight different 'Fragments' published by The Bystander of which over a million copies were sold. Later, he became editor of his own weekly Fragments magazine which proved as successful.

Many historical ties unite Belgium and the United Kingdom. At the time of the publication of the first volume of 'Fragments from France' Belgium was occupied by Germany and heavy fighting was taking place, particularly in the area around Ypres in the South Western corner of the country. The gallantry with which the Belgian army fought under King Albert I, aroused both admiration and sympathy. Nowhere was this more evident than in Britain: committees were formed, funds raised, meetings held, books and articles published. After the war the heroism of Brave Little Belgium was acknowledged in the fact that Belgium is the only non-Commonwealth country whose armed forces are allowed to bear arms at the yearly Cenotaph parade held each year in London in July, a privilege granted by King George V.

The majority of Bairnsfather's war-time cartoons are set in Northern France and South West Belgium. Since Belgium is often regarded as the home of cartoons and comic strip art, it is entirely appropriate for me as Belgian Ambassador to the UK, to host this occasion. To mark the 50th anniversary of Bairnsfather's death and in support of the charity Help For Heroes (H4H), Pen and Sword Books are publishing some 140 of the artist's cartoons in this reprint Best of Fragments From France. I am pleased to be able to contribute to both this homage to the British artist and the charity H4H which supports wounded British servicemen and women returning from Afghanistan and Iraq. Do you know "a better hole" than this for your money?

Valmai Holt with the Belgian Ambassador, Jean-Michel Veranneman de Watervliet, at the annual dinner of the Guild of Battlefield Guides.

Jean-Michel Veranneman de Watervliet
The Ambassador of H.M. The King of the Belgians

INTRODUCTION TO THE "BB4H4H" EDITION OF
BEST OF FRAGMENTS FROM FRANCE
50th Anniversary of the death of Captain Bruce Bairnsfather

Bruce Bairnsfather (BB) was the most famous cartoonist of the First World War and his soldier characters Old Bill, Bert and Alf, faced with sardonic good humour everything that the Germans, the mud and their officers could throw at them. However, Bruce (known by some as 'The Man Who Won the War') never received the acclaim that he deserved for the morale boost that his cartoons gave to the troops at the front and to the people back at home. The 50th Anniversary of Bairnsfather's death on 29 September 2009 offered an opportunity to redress the balance, and acknowledging it in combination with raising funds for **Help for Heroes** (H4H) seemed to be most appropriate.

In October 2007 Bryn and Emma Parry founded H4H, a charity devoted to providing support for our service men and women wounded, both mentally and physically, in Iraq and Afghanistan who, many felt, were not being well enough cared for when they returned home. Thus, in a way, there is a thematic link between the two - Bruce in '14-'18 not properly appreciated and our wounded from recent conflicts apparently not properly cared for.

During the war the British soldier and civilian had shared a common bond - a sense of humour. They had an extraordinary ability to laugh at themselves, at each other, at their misfortunes and even the terrors of war itself. They laughed at the enemy, too, but with a tolerant good humour, more in ridicule than in the virulent spite that ran through their French and German counterparts. This humour kept them going, no matter how bad things became and kept them together, good-humoured through the common adversity, until the end, until they won.

The character who, more than any other in the Great War, stimulated and prolonged this unique ability to keep morale high through laughter was known as 'Old Bill'. Born in the mud of 'Plugstreet Wood' on the slopes of the Messines Ridge near Ypres in November 1914, Old Bill, of the walrus moustache, muffler and balaclava, became as recognisable a personage as that other famous man of the people, Charlie Chaplin. He was the archetypal British Civilian - who just happened to find himself in the centre of the greatest holocaust the world had ever known. He coped with it equally, refusing to be ruffled, always ready with a bon mot or a quip. So dramatic was the morale effect of the cartoons that Bairnsfather was transferred to the Intelligence Department and lent in turn to the French, the Italians and the Americans.

The situation of the most famous of all the Fragments, **The Better 'Ole**, shown on the cover, has been used by many public figures, (including Roosevelt and Chamberlain), often to make a political points and there have been innumerable cartoons published in the national press by the leading cartoonists of the day inspired by BB's famous 'Ole: Brooke, Breeze, Chat, Cummings, Garland, Illingworth, Jensen, Matt, Mahood, ...

Between the two World Wars Bruce Bairnsfather and Old Bill became international stars. Their prowess, their fame and their decline is traced in detail in our biography, **In Search of the Better 'Ole**. There were lectures, plays, films, books, magazines, articles, strip cartoons, television programmes in which they appeared, many items of merchandise - from shaving mugs to car mascots – and celebrities from Houdini to Hitler that they met in their world-wide travels.

During World War Two Bairnsfather served with the U.S.A.A.F. as official laughter-maker. But apart from producing a couple of posters for wartime magazines like the *Royal British Legion* Journal and *Defence*, he was little used by the British. After the War, Bairnsfather lived quietly, moving from cottage to cottage, painting country landscapes and doing one-night guest appearances at local functions. His popularity as an international, even as a national, figure waned, mainly because he never could release the stranglehold that Old Bill had on him, obscuring his talent as a serious artist. So the very cause of Bairnsfather's incredible success was also his Achilles heel and the success of The Better 'Ole led to the 'Ole in which he was firmly stuck for the rest of his life.

Our first edition of Best of Fragments from France was published in 1978 when an element of our Royalties went to the Royal British Legion. With this edition all of our Royalties will go to H4H. This will not only help the charity but also bring Bruce's work to the attention of an audience that is today increasingly interested in the events of '14 –'18. Charles Hewitt, the Managing Director of Pen and Sword Books, agreed to publish the book and we are most grateful to him for that support.

When we were doing our research on Bairnsfather back in the 1970s we asked the major cartoonists of the day to draw their version of The Better 'Ole for us. This time, thanks to the enthusiastic support of Oliver Preston and Anita O'Brian of the Cartoon Art Museum, a number of today's leading cartoonists have drawn a cartoon - some inspired by Bairnsfather - and have donated it to an auction at the Museum at 1700 hours on Tuesday 29 September 2009. Those cartoons are republished in this book. We are also donating the *Better Ole* cartoon drawn for us by Cummings.

Someone who gave immediate support to us from the moment that we had the idea was H.E. Jean-Michel Veranneman de Watervliet, the Belgian Ambassador, and we are most grateful to him for offering to hold the launch of the book at his Residence in London and for writing the Foreword to this edition.

We have also arranged a small ceremony on 3 October 2009 at the BB plaque in St Yvon to mark the 50th Anniversary, and the Burgomaster of Comines-Warneton has fully supported the event. Mark Warby, Editor of *The Old Bill Newsletter*, and dedicated BB supporter, has created a tour to coincide with the commemoration.

These and other events to publicise the book's connection with Help For Heroes we call our BB4H4H campaign and ongoing details about the auction, the book and the tour can be found at:

www.bb4h4h.co.uk

Tonie and Valmai Holt
Woodnesborough, 2009

There are many others to thank for their much-appreciated support. They are acknowledged later in this book.

THE ORIGINAL *FRAGMENTS*

The cartoons reproduced in this collection were originally drawn for *The Bystander*, a popular weekly magazine, in which they appeared each Tuesday throughout most of the Great War. Their effect on the public was totally unexpected, and so dramatic that *Bystander* sales soared. The organisation, with unerring good judgement, decided it had a winner in Bairnsfather, and published the first 43 of his cartoons in an anthology. It was produced in February 1916, given the name *Fragments from France* and sold for 1s. On the front cover was a coloured print of *The Better 'Ole* which soon became, and was to remain, the most loved of all Bairnsfather's cartoons. The authors own the original.

Sales quickly reached a quarter of a million and a second anthology was published, *More Fragments from France*. It was described on the title page as 'Vol II' and the price was still 1s. The cartoon on the cover was *What time do they feed the sea lions?*

In this volume *The Bystander* launched the first of a series of imaginative marketing exercises, similar to modern promotional methods for later winning products such as 'Snoopy', 'The Wombles', 'Jaws', 'E.T.' and the robot 'Artoo Detoo' from 'Star Wars'. They advertised coloured prints of a selection of the cartoons published in the first volume. The full extent of the proliferation of the cartoons on all manner of products, from playing cards to pottery, is described in our Bairnsfather biography.

Soon *Still More Fragments from France* were clamoured for, and, with an eye to the future, the booklet was labelled No. 3 on the cover, Vol III on the title page. The cartoon on the cover was *Let's 'ave this pin of yours a minute.*

The marketing of Bairnsfather and Old Bill took a step forward in this volume. In it were advertisements for:

"BAIRNSFATHER". A few Fragments from his Life. Fifty Original Sketches. Post Free 4/-.

BULLETS AND BILLETS. Bairnsfather's Life at the Front. Forty Original Sketches. Post Free 5/6

FRAGMENTS PLAYING CARDS. Many Subjects. Per Pack, post free 1/9.

FRAGMENTS Edition de Luxe. Specially suitable for presentation. Post Free 5/6.

FRAGMENTS FROM FRANCE. Volumes I and II. Post Free 1/3 each.

In the foreword to *Number Four*, the Editor of *The Bystander* wrote, "Just as umpty years ago, people used to look forward with an almost greedy anxiety to the day when the next monthly part of *The Pickwick Papers* in its green paper cover, was due to appear, so now they worry the bookstall newsvendors to know when the next volume of *Fragments* will be ready".

On the last page of the booklet were the words, "This issue completes a volume. Binding Cases 2/4, post free from the Publisher". *Number Four* was still 1/- net and had a cartoon *Keep away from the 'ive Bert* on the cover..

No. 5 went up to 1/6 net and had a different design on the front cover — a large '5' with Old Bill's head smiling through

it. For the first time there was no foreword by the Editor, simply a full page picture of 'BB'.

Volumes 1-5 develop the archetypal characters of Old Bill, Bert, Alf and Col. Chutney and their ilk in situations almost exclusively drawn from Bairnsfather's own experience as a soldier on the British Sector of the Western Front. The bulk of them were produced whilst he was convalescing at the family home at Bishopton, near Stratford-upon-Avon, from a wound received during the first German gas attack in the 1st Battle of Ypres in April 1915. While still in hospital prior to his leave at Bishopton he had been visited by 'a representative of *The Bystander*', who told him of the astounding success of the first cartoons and encouraged him to submit more. 'Well I'm d—d!' commented Bruce to his mother. 'Fancy them wanting some more drawings.'

Volume 6, produced towards the end of the War, reflects Lt. Bairnsfather's promotion to Captain and elevation to the Intelligence Department. It recorded his missions to the French, Italian and American Fronts and is a jolly sketch book of the *Poilu*, his Italian counterpart and the American Doughboy at War. It was *Number Six* and was entitled *Fragments from All the Fronts*. Again, there is no foreword, but a 'snapshot of Captain Bairnsfather taken during one of his visits to the American Army in France'. This photograph is reproduced on page 132 of this selection.

Number Seven went back to the original cover design, with a coloured cartoon of Old Bill in pink and red camouflage stripes. The original of this cartoon is in the Imperial War Museum. The 7th Volume of Fragments was produced after the Armistice, but before the Peace Treaty of Versailles had been signed in July 1919. It comments on Peacetime, demobilisation and the Army of Occupation. It has a foreword by The Bystander Editor, who described it as 'a link between those glorious achievements on the Western Front that culminated at 5a.m. on November 11, 1918 and the events which so swiftly followed that historic date'.

Number Eight (Completing the Second Volume) had a cartoon of a stone colossus Old Bill on the cover. It traced the development of *Old Bill Through The Ages* and commented on the current political and topical scene — from Bolshevism to jazz and profiteering. It was the last volume.

The success of the *Fragments* magazines was such that edition followed edition in rapid succession and at least eleven editions were published.

The covers retained the same cartoon but were reproduced in different colours, both of board and ink — green, blue, red, grey, fawn and mauve. In America Putnam's issued Nos. I-IV as one volume and parts V and VI separately. Various hard and leather-bound collections were offered for sale by *The Bystander*, and the drawings were sold separately as prints and "Portfolios" for framing. They were also printed in colour as give-aways for *Answers* magazine.

Leafing through these pages, the reader will soon understand their tremendous popularity and success which have withstood the test of time.

PAGE INDEX TO *FRAGMENTS* CAPTIONS

"Where did that one go to?"

This is the very first 'Fragment'. It was conceived in November 1914 in the trenches at 'Plugstreet Wood' (Tommy's name for the Bois de Ploegsteert) near Messines in the Ypres Salient. Bruce Bairnsfather was then a 2nd Lieutenant serving in the Royal Warwickshire Regiment. The cartoon is based on a real situation experienced by Bairnsfather, using 'a sentence which must have been said countless times in this War', for the caption. The finished drawing was completed sometime in January 1915 whilst the artist was enjoying a rest period in his billet, a cottage at St Yvon. He sent it to 'The Bystander' a copy of which was still 'lying about' after Christmas. It was accepted, reproduced in 'The Bystander' on 31 March 1915 and they paid the fee of 3 Guineas for it! Bairnsfather first saw the printed cartoon when convalescing in hospital at Rouen in May 1915, when it was pointed out to him by a fellow patient.

"They've evidently seen me"

This cartoon was the second 'Fragment'. Bairnsfather had first drawn the idea for this sketch on the walls of an old cottage in St Yvon just behind the Front Line. He then redrew it for a Major Lancaster (who was killed on 8 May 1915 in the first gas attack at Ypres: Major John Cecil Lancaster who is buried in Oostaverne Wood Cemetery). Finally he did a colour wash and sent it to 'The Bystander' on 9 April 1915.

'I hope it will meet with your approval', he wrote in his covering letter. 'Although I do not observe from a chimney myself, yet at the present time I happen to 'live' in a house. By 'live' I mean waiting for the next shell to come through the roof.' 'The Bystander' paid 2 Guineas for the cartoon. This is the cartoon that we reproduced in 2003 on the bronze memorial plaque that we placed on the rebuilt cottage in St Yvon.

Situation Shortly Vacant

In an old-fashioned house in France an opening will shortly occur for a young man, with good prospects of getting a rise

---

Bert has a good idea where this shell is going to land! Note the pun on the word 'rise'. Bairnsfather was very fond of puns and in the weekly magazine called 'Fragments' that he edited in 1919 and 1920 he ran regular Pun Competitions. The results were excruciating.

The Tactless Teuton

A member of the Gravediggers' Corps joking with a private in the
Orphans' Battalion, prior to a frontal attack

---

*As Vivian Carter, Editor of 'The Bystander', pointed out, when Bairnsfather wished to make a 'slightly brutal'
comment he 'fathers it upon the enemy'. Old Bill would never be so heartless. Note, too, how Bairnsfather has
captured everyman's concept of how a German should look. In May 1916 a German officer wrote to 'The
Bystander': 'Compliments to Captain Bairnsfather and we should like him to know that we are so pleased to
provide a source of innocent amusement in the shrinking tendency of our forage caps and the generous
dimensions of our waist measurements. Alas, that there should exist degenerate exceptions! My personal 'outer
man' lacks both these endearing characteristics. I feel quite an imposter.'*

Coiffure in the Trenches

"Keep yer 'ead still, or I'll 'ave yer blinkin' ear off"

The basic function of life had to continue during trench warfare – eating, sleeping, drinking, washing and, of course in the British Army, hair cutting. Perhaps Bairnsfather was here replying to his critic, a columnist in 'The Times' newspaper, who castigated him thus, 'Nothing so quickly lowers moral as slovenliness, and nothing is more difficult to check than the gradual degeneration due to trench life and yet we have an Army officer who invariably depicts his men as the very type the Army is anxious to suppress'. One of Bairnsfather's most vivid memories of the 1914 Christmas Truce was 'a vision of one of my machine gunners, who was a bit of an amateur hairdresser in civil life, cutting the unnaturally long hair of a docile Boche'. In 2008 a memorial to the Christmas Truce was unveiled at Frelinghien on the French/Belgian border. The Khaki Chums also erected a memorial cross to the truce at St Yvon in 2003.

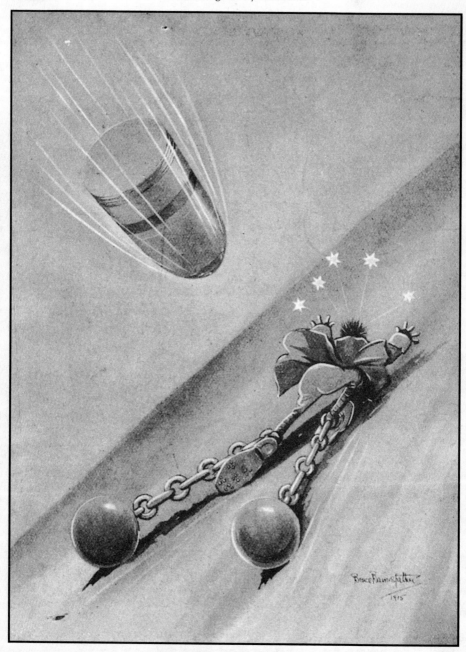

"That 16-inch Sensation"

During his weeks of convalescence after his injury in April 1915, Bairnsfather had many recurring nightmares about his experiences. 'During these days my mind seemed to be going through the War again - about twice nightly – in my dreams.

I think everyone who gets 'knocked out' knows this sensation of 'fighting one's battle over again'. His own injury at Ypres was caused by a shell burst. '16-inch' refers to the size of the shell. The German 'Big Bertha', for instance, was this size.

No Possible Doubt Whatever

Sentry: "'Alt! Who goes there?"
He of the Bundle: "You shut yer ——— mouth, or I'll ——— come
    and knock yer ——— head off!"
Sentry: "Pass, friend!"

It was cartoons like this, that show Bairnsfather's total identification with, and understanding for, the British soldier's spirit and language, which brought certain criticisms upon the artist. According to the Editor of 'The Bystander', an 'eminent political personage' thought Capt. Bairnsfather should 'avoid casting ridicule at the British Army, or giving the impression that it was less serious of purpose than the armies of the other Allies'

"Gott strafe this barbed wire"

'Gott Strafe (God Punish) England' became a standard German propaganda slogan and was used as a daily greeting between friends and to open telephone conversations. Tommy quickly picked up the phrase and 'strafed' anything that annoyed him, from Staff Officers to the endless issues of plum and apple jam.

What it Really Feels Like

To be on patrol duty at night-time

Anyone who has ever been out alone at night knows that every shadow hides a threat and every sound a danger. Every soldier who has stood on night duty, or patrolled in the dark knows the feeling this cartoon expresses – that the enemy is everywhere. The threatening oppression which surrounds the lonely soldier in the dark never totally left Bairnsfather. 'To me the... horrible reality of this terribly elementary and brutal War, was burning a hole in my mind and system, which time can never heal.'

15

That Sword

How he thought he was going to use it—

—and how he did use it

The days of dashing cavalry charges and derring-do were soon buried for ever by the murderous fire of the machine gun, and in the mundane life of bogged-down trench warfare that developed after the Retreat from Mons. Visions of chivalrous inspiration translated into the boring business of survival. Bairnsfather captures reality with humour, an abrupt contrast to the idealised drawings of a Harry Payne or Caton-Woodville.

" Well, if you knows of a better 'ole, go to it "

This is Bairnsfather's most famous cartoon. It was drawn after he was injured during the Second Battle of Ypres and following a period of recuperation on the Isle of Wight. When the cartoon was published in the Christmas 1915 edition of 'The Bystander' the public, to use the words of a contemporary commentator, 'collapsed'. 'If you knows of a better 'ole' and variations of the phrase have been the title of stage shows, films and radio shows. Pubs, restaurants and hotels have carried the name and even in 1978 there was a restaurant called 'The Better 'Ole', well-known to British soldiers, in Fanling on the border of Communist China and Hong Kong. The original Bairnsfather drawing was bought by an un-named War Office General and the artist, who said 'I did not think so much of this drawing', was paid 4 Guineas for it by 'The Bystander'. The authors own the original drawing.

The Things that Matter

Scene : Loos, during the September offensive.

Colonel Fitz-Shrapnel receives the following message from ''G.H.Q.'':—
''Please let us know, as soon as possible, the number of tins of raspberry jam issued to you last Friday''

When the war settled down into its trenches, systems of supply for everything from food through clothing to ammunition had to be developed to meet the needs of the millions of men at war. As the administrative tail of the fighting army grew in size and began to wag the dog, the number of returns for supplies that Commanding Officers had to produce became so numerous that Colonel Fitz-Shrapnel may well have found himself in this situation. The puzzle is – how did he manage to get RASPBERRY jam?

So Obvious

The Young and Talkative One: "Who made that 'ole?"
The Fed-up One: "Mice"

The Germans decided that Tommy's sense of humour was a major factor in maintaining morale and attempted to instil a similar sense of humour into their own troops. It is said that they used this cartoon to illustrate a manual on humour and in order to ensure that the message got across, they added, with Teutonic thoroughness, the following note, 'It was not mice. It was a shell.' In WW2 when Bairnsfather was the cartoonist to the US 8th Airforce a Flying Fortress returning from a mission had a large hole in the tail rudder and he updated this cartoon.

The Fatalist

"I'm sure they'll 'ear this damn thing squeakin'"

Bairnsfather explains: 'He (the fatalist) knows the water has to be drawn and that he is responsible for drawing it, but he does think it a cruel world which makes the filling of a mere jar of water – water, mind you, not rum, or anything really worth dying for – such a dangerous proceeding... he doesn't like the prospect of meeting his end because a 'damned pump' squeaks. All pumps in Flanders squeak, and if this 'Fragment' had a lot of success, it's because every man in Northern France was perfectly sure it was the particular pump he had experienced himself. I had heaps of letters claiming the pump.'

"There goes our blinkin' parapet again"

Written in the Douve area, near St Yvon: 'Persistent shelling of the left hand end of our trenches meant a persistent readjustment of our parapets, and putting things back again. Each morning the Boches would knock the things down and each evening we would put them up again. Our soldiers are only amused at this procedure... On several evenings I had to go round and arrange for the reconstruction of the ruined parapet or squashed-in dugouts. It was during one of these little episodes that I felt the spirit of my drawing, 'There goes our blinkin' parapet again'.'

The Thirst for Reprisals

"'And me a rifle, someone. I'll give these ——— s 'ell for this!''

Bairnsfather explains: 'The figure under the debris feels for the first time that full spirit of hate for the enemy...
the War has just been brought home to him... If the British public had the War brought home to them in the
same way, they'd feel the same thing, and the trouble is that they haven't, except where the Zepps fly, and in
consequence they don't feel the War.'

Keeping His Hand In

Private Smith, the company bomber, formerly "Shinio," the popular
juggler, frequently causes considerable anxiety to his platoon

---

The serious point underlying the humour of this
cartoon is the many hours of idleness and boredom
that the troops had to endure in the unpleasant
discomfort of the trenches. There would have been
ample time and opportunity to practice many skills
and postal courses in everything from 'Sketching' or
'Self-Improvement' (e.g. Pelmanism) were sold to the
troops. Bairnsfather tackles this same theme with
other artistes, including a tight-rope walker on the
barbed wire.

23

Note that the rations consist of rum and hard dry biscuits. Bairnsfather's harsh reviewer in 'The Times' commented, 'Readers of Mr Wells' last book will remember the Cockney soldier of the new army who could not open his mouth without using the word 'bloody', not because he liked it, but because Ortheris, his beau ideal of a soldier, did so, and the disgust that he aroused in his fellow-soldiers who preferred – shall we say Wordsworth's ideal? We know a battalion where a soldier such as Captain Bairnsfather takes as his type would be summarily dealt with'. It may have been views like this amongst the High Command that prevented Bairnsfather from being properly recognised for his contribution to morale.

" ———— these ———— rations "

The Innocent Abroad

Out since Mons: "Well, what sort of a night 'ave yer 'ad?"
Novice (but persistent optimist): "Oh, alright. 'Ad to get out and rest a bit
    now and again"

'Out since Mons' refers to the small band of the original British Expeditionary Force of professional soldiers sent out to France in August 1914. They were referred to by the Kaiser as that 'Contemptible Little Army' and henceforward proudly bore the nickname of 'Old Contemptibles'. They delayed the German General von Kluck's aggressive advance through Belgium by their heroic stand at Mons, though greatly outnumbered. This was followed by The Great Retreat.

25

"The Spirit of our Troops is Excellent"

The spirit referred to is rum, which was issued to troops as part of their rations to warm and cheer them up in the damp and cold of the trenches. It was particularly efficacious in the chilly dawn period just before 'going over the top' to fortify them before an attack. In the half light, soldiers often got away with queuing up for a second tot. As a double ration was normally issued before 'going over the top', Tommy got to associate the bringing up of the rum jar with an imminent attack. On the rum jars was stencilled the letters SRD which stood for 'Services Rum Distribution' but to Tommy in the trenches they meant 'Seldom Reaches Destination'.

Our Democratic Army

Member of Navvies' Battalion (to Colonel): "I say, yer mate's
dropped 'is cane"

Democracy only began to creep into the British Army in WW1 when the young Subalterns shared the privations of their men and, perhaps for the first time, began to understand and appreciate them. The gap, however, was particularly wide between front-line officers and Staff Officers who, with Headquarters several miles behind the Front Line, often had no conception of the real conditions in which men lived and fought.

FINIS

When the young officer came home on leave he indulged in a furious round of theatre going, dining in restaurants and night clubbing. The new jazz music had arrived from America and hundreds of night clubs sprang up in and around London together with hordes of what Bairnsfather called 'dubious women'. Special squads of women police were recruited to patrol known trouble spots like the Strand, which they called 'The Devil's Promenade'. 'Khaki Fever' was rampant and drunkenness and illegitimacy boomed.

Leave

The young officer has a far away look in his eyes. It was hard to make the transition form the hell of the trenches to the relative normality of civilian life. A great gulf existed between the soldier and civilian because the latter could not grasp the enormity of the horror that the former lived through every day under battle conditions.

"How long have you got Fred?"

" LEAVE "

Many soldiers never came back. The chances were that Fred's wife would soon be a widow. Nearly every family in the land suffered bereavement and the women were called upon to do jobs previously only open to men. The widening of women's roles during the war did much to promote the cause of women's suffrage, and in 1918 women over 30 had the Vote. Here Bairnsfather shows the soldier's hands. He wasn't good at drawing hands and generally did his best to conceal them.

Those Tubular Trenches

" Is this right for 'eadquarters ? "
" Yes, change at Oxford Circus "

Old Bill and Bert are now wearing tin helmets which were not issued until the Battle of Hooge in July 1915. Before that date our heroes are shown wearing their Balaclavas or soft peaked caps. Much of the War took place underground with railway systems, huge subterranean caverns large enough to hold a Battalion, hospital and kitchen areas. The tunnel system under Vimy Ridge, scene of the great Canadian triumph in April 1917, can still be visited, as can those dug by New Zealand tunnellers at Arras.

31

"My dream for years to come"

This particular cartoon is the artist's true personal nightmare. Profoundly disturbed by the horror of war he undoubtedly experienced what was euphemistically known as 'shell shock' when he was blown up by a shell at Wieltje near Ypres. His first leave in April 1915, after 6 months in the trenches, was extended after a medical examination. The War seemed to alter his whole personality permanently – from a mischievous prankster to the shy, solitary character he remained up to his lonely death in 1959.

A Maxim Maxim

"Fire should be withheld till a favourable target presents itself"

Another Bairnsfather pun: Maxim, as in gun, and maxim, as in 'a general principle, serving as a rule or guide'. Bairnsfather was himself a machine-gun officer and in the early days along the Messines Ridge his guns were indeed Maxims – which he called 'a very weighty concern.' He described his job thus, 'Mostly improving machine-gun positions, or selecting new sites and carrying out removals:

BRUCE BAIRNSFATHER

MACHINE GUNS REMOVED AT SHORT NOTICE

ATTACKS QUOTED FOR'

Another Maxim Maxim

"Machine guns form a valuable support for infantry"

It was a favourite pastime of both sides during the Great War to accuse the enemy of drunkenness. The Germans in their turn produced many propaganda cartoons depicting the Russians as alcoholics. During the German offensive of March 1918 Rudolph Binding, the German writer, recalled seeing his 'men carrying a bottle of wine under their arm and another open in their hand... men staggering... men who could hardly walk.'

"The same old moon"

A double sketch which underlined the chasm that existed between civilians – with their romantic notions of the glamour of 'going forth to war' – and Tommies who had to live the unglamorous and dangerous reality. The wiring party's job was always dangerous in moonlit conditions when alert German snipers had a clear target. Old Bill and his companion are using wooden posts to hold the barbed wire. Later on, metal rods twisted into a screw shape were produced and these can still be seen being used as fence posts on the battlefields today. Wiring parties also laid wire for field telephones.

35

Tactical Developments

Private ⁵998 Blobs has always thought a machine for imitating the sound of ration parties (and thus drawing fire) an excellent idea, but simply hates his evening for working it

Bairnsfather in a technical mood, more typical of Heath Robinson or Searle. He was very aware that the lot of the rationing party was not a happy one. 'Think of the rottenest, wettest, windiest winter's night you can remember and add to it this bleak, muddy, war-worn plain with its ruined farms and shell-torn lonely road. Then think of men, leaving the trenches at dusk going back about a mile and a half, and bringing sundry large and heavy boxes up to the trenches pausing now and again for a rest and ignoring the intermittent crackling of rifle fire in the darkness and the sharp 'phut' of bullets biting the mud all around.'

No " Light " Call

" Bert, 'ere's the man about the gas"

Many types of gas were experimented with during the Great War. Chlorine was the first, used by the Germans at St Julien on French Colonial Turco troops in April 1915. Mustard gas was probably the most noxious as it caused burns and blisters to the skin as well as causing internal injury. The Germans introduced it in the Summer of 1917.

That "Out Wiring" Sensation

'That moonlight feeling is very curious. You feel as if the enemy can see you clearly and that all eyes in the opposite trench are turned on you. You can almost imagine a Boche smilingly taking an aim, and saying to a friend, "We'll just let him come a bit closer first".'

That Provost-Marshal Feeling

A sensation only to be had at a Base—in other words, a base sensation

One of Bairnsfather's comparatively rare female studies, which comments upon the 'no fraternisation' rule. He was particularly observant about female fashions and before the War often enjoyed playing female parts in pantomimes and entertainments at Bishopton and Stratford. His mother made some of his costumes and lady friends provided others. 'R---n' is, of course, ROUEN. Bairnsfather had a run-in with a Provost-Marshal in the Adelphi Hotel in Liverpool in 1918 when he was accused of 'acting in a manner prejudicial to our winning the War' by wearing black socks with brown shoes.

39

Blighty!

The word 'Blighty' is reputed to have come from the British Army's days in India – a derivation of the Hindustani word 'bilayat' meaning 'own district'.

Thus the UK came to be known as 'Dear Old Blighty' and to get a 'Blighty one' meant to be wounded seriously enough to be sent home for treatment.

Down at the Base Camp

"'E 'as to pick up odd bits of paper and match-ends down the camp, sir ; but 'e don't seem to 'ave 'is 'eart in 's work, sir!"

Anyone who has been the object of a British Sergeant's scathing remarks will know exactly how our soldier feels. Once in the Front Line, such niceties as picking up match ends had be abandoned and the men lived in the trenches amidst the most unpleasant debris – from the corpses of their comrades, which often formed an integral part of the trench wall, to rusty cans from their ration packs. Bairnsfather upset many senior officers by showing the battlefields as they really were – full of tin cans and other rubbish. Perhaps another reason why officialdom did not reward his talent.

A.D. Nineteen Fifty

"I see the War Babies' Battalion is a coming out"

At first the opinion was unanimously held by both sides that the War would be all over by Christmas of 1914. When it dragged on into its fourth year with little ground lost or won by either side, it must have seemed a permanent condition to the few hardened soldiers who survived from the beginning.

Frustrated Ingenuity

Owing to dawn breaking sooner than he anticipated, that inventive fellow, Private Jones, has a trying time with his latest creation, "The Little Plugstreet," the sniper's friend

The idea used in this scene cropped again many years later in Bairnsfather's career. In 1927 Charlie Chaplin was being sued by the author of 'The Rookie' for using the latter's ideas in a film Charlie called 'Shoulder Arms'. In it Chaplin, as a Private in the War, disguises himself as a tree to evade his German pursuers. Bairnsfather acted as a witness on Chaplin's behalf, and during the hearing showed the court how he had originated this idea in 'Fragments'. Chaplin won the case.

Basil Rathbone, the stage and film actor famous for playing Sherlock Holmes, served with the London Scottish during the War and recalled doing exactly what the cartoon depicts. 'We brought back an awful lot of information', he remarked.

The Eternal Question

"When the 'ell is it goin' to be strawberry?"

The complaints that Tommy made about the inferior quality of tinned rations and the profiteering of certain manufacturers was often justified. Plum and apple jam became a symbol for second best, but it was better than the sawdust and chalk that German civilians had to resort to eating when the British blockade started to take effect.

Thoroughness

Like Colonel Chutney, Bairnsfather preferred not to break with the rigours of trench life when engaged in war. He feared that the adjustment to a softer life, and then back again, would be harder to make than the continuance of the hardship. He often turned down comrades' invitations to spend the evening carousing in an estaminet behind the lines. This self-enforced endurance took its toll and Bairnsfather was several times reduced to a state of exhaustion and over-strain.

" Dear ——

"At present we are staying at a farm . . . "

As the Editor of 'The Bystander' writes, 'Captain Bruce Bairnsfather has stayed at that 'farm'... he has endured that shell-swept 'ole... had his hair cut under fire... and having been through it all, he has just put down what he has seen and heard and felt and smelt and – laughed at.' Bairnsfather was as horrified at the devastation to the countryside and livestock as he was at the loss of human life. Less than a kilometre to the east of Bairnsfather's cottage at St Yvon is a farm that is still called 'Dead Cow Farm.'

Directing the Way at the Front

"Yer knows the dead 'orse 'cross the road ? Well, keep straight on till, yer comes to a p'rambulator 'longside a Johnson 'ole"

Because of the heavy bombardment from both sides, landmarks like trees or houses disappeared from the landscape with alarming rapidity. Dead horses and Johnson holes often stayed around longer. A Johnson hole is one made by a shell from a German heavy gun which, on bursting, gave out a cloud of thick black smoke. Tommy associated the black smoke with the well-known negro boxer Jack Johnson and hence – 'Johnson hole'. Political correctness had not yet been invented.

The Dud Shell — Or the Fuse-Top Collector

" Give it a good 'ard 'un, Bert ; you can generally 'ear 'em fizzing a bit first
if they are a-goin' to explode "

*Despite regulations forbidding it, souvenirs were avidly collected by Tommy to take home as trophies of war.
As well as fuse tops, any kind of German headgear was eagerly scrambled for – in particular the spiked
pickelhaube. Bert is trying to remove the nose cap fuse from the shell. Even today such shells are found on the
battlefield and unwise individuals try to remove the nose cap with the result that from time to time there are
accidents and even fatalities should the shell explode. If you visit the battlefields it is best not to pick up
anything.*

That Hat

" Pop out and get it, Bert "
" Pop out yerself "

'The Times Literary Supplement' of 21 December 1916: 'It is not with Captain Bairnstather's humour that we quarrel, for his situations are invariably amusing. It is because he standardises – almost idealises – a depraved type of face. We cannot but enter a protest against so cruel a caricature of the men who endured the first winter in France. The men we knew jested and swore like many other gallant men, but they prided themselves on being the smartest in the Brigade, not the one that most resembled one of Bairnsfather's drawings.'

The New Submarine Danger

" They'll be torpedoin' us if we stick 'ere much longer, Bill "

'I never went about looking for ideas for drawings; the whole business of the War seemed to come before me in a series of pictures. Jokes used to stick out of all the horrible discomfort, something like the points of a harrow would stick into you if you slept on it.'

When One Would Like to Start an Offensive on One's Own

RECIPE FOR FEELING LIKE THIS—Bully, biscuits, no coke, and leave just cancelled

---

Despite the circumstances, this seems a comparatively well-equipped dugout – firmly sand-bagged, dry and sheltered enough to keep the candle alight and with the space for drying socks. Keeping the feet dry was one of the biggest problems of trench life. Constant immersion in water made the feet swell so much that the skin burst, a painful condition known as 'Trench Foot'. The coke referred to is of the burning variety, not the drinking or snorting.

Trouble With One of the Souvenirs

" 'Old these a minute while I takes that blinkin' smile off 'is dial "

When life was particularly hot and casualties alarmingly high, the willingness of German soldiers to be taken prisoner in the hopes of then surviving the War was often noted. Bairnsfather was a great souvenir collector himself. When his first leave came through his main concern was his 'heavy bag of souvenirs.' One package had four 'Little Willie' cases inside, (the cast-iron shell cases for the German equivalent of our 18-pounders). The haversack was filled with aluminium fuse tops and one large piece of a 'Jack Johnson' shell case.

A Matter of Moment

"What was that, Bill?"
"Trench mortar"
"Ours or theirs?"

It was inevitable, when the big guns on either side were finding their range on a new target, that shells would sometimes fall short and land on their own troops. The worst incidents were during the 'creeping barrages' that often preceded a big attack (such as the Battle of the Somme in July 1916). During such a barrage the men had to walk forward at a certain speed and, theoretically, the shells from their supporting barrage would move ahead of them at the same speed. It was frequently impossible to keep to the rigid schedule and many men were wiped out in this way, cursing their own gunners. Later this tragedy, which occurs in most battle conditions, would euphemistically be called 'Friendly Fire' or 'Blue on Blue'.

The Historical Touch

" Well, Alfred, 'ow are the cakes?"

While at school Bairnsfather recounted how he was probably the most caned boy there. One weekend he was given an extra caning because he had had so many canings during the week. During lessons he spent a great deal of time drawing caricatures of the boys and masters, for which he was generally punished. Perhaps he is letting his history teacher know here that he did absorb some facts...

'Ensign' wrote in 'The Outlook', "You may have possibly seen Captain Bruce Bairnsfather's two inimitable pictures depicting the hour before going into trenches and the hour after coming out. Well, they are absolutely IT. Lord how we laughed over them in the front line; and mind you, I am not puffing Bairnsfather: he does not need it, but take it from me he is one of the people who by supplying roars of laughter and joy to the troops are helping to win the war."

In and Out (I)

That last half-hour before "going in" to the same trenches for the 200th time

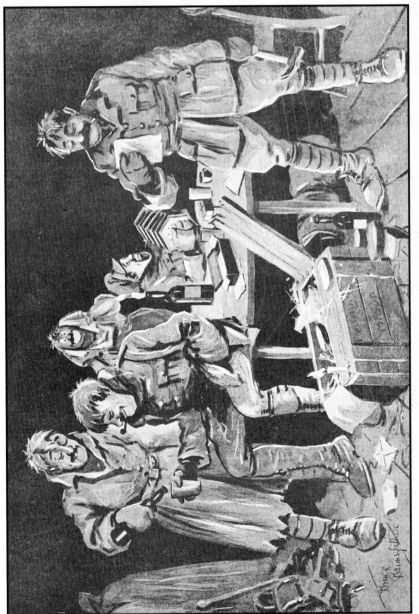

In and Out (II)

That first half-hour after "coming out" of those same trenches

His Secret Sorrow

"I reckon this bloke must 'ave caught 'is face against some of them forts at Verdun!"

It was at Verdun, with its famous fortresses, that the German General von Falkenhayen chose to wage his war of attrition, hoping to bleed the French white. He knew that the French would pour ever more troops in to hold this symbol of French pride. But for almost every Frenchman that died, so did a German. The French lost 315,000 casualties, the Germans 281,000. The conditions at Verdun were appalling, the guns deafening, the ground churned into a sort of lunar landscape. But the French held out, and Tommy admired them for it.

The Professional Touch

" Chuck us out that bag o' bombs, mate ; it's under your 'ead "

Bert has the ubiquitous cigarette hanging from his lips. Many Fund-Raising schemes to keep the troops supplied with tobacco were instigated. Most famous was Princess Mary's Fund which at Christmas time in 1914 provided the familiar brass boxes containing tobacco. The proceeds of the sale of postcards of popular entertainers also went to a tobacco fund organised by the 'Weekly Despatch'. Bairnsfather talks of his 'usual copious supply of Gold Flake cigarettes, of which during my life in France, I must have consumed several army corps.'

The Conscientious Exhilarator

" Every encouragement should be given for singing and whistling."—(Extract from a " Military Manual.")

That painstaking fellow, Lieut. Orpheus, does his best, but finds it uphill work at times

The chances are that Lieut. Orpheus is whistling 'It's a long way to Tipperary'. It was the hit song of the war. Composed by a market stall holder, Jack Judge, it was taken up by the Germans as well as the Allies – much as 'Lili Marlene' was popular on both sides in WW2. The French and Belgians often used it as an alternative British national anthem to 'God Save the King'.

The Intelligence Department

" Is this 'ere the Warwicks ? "
" Nao, 'Indenburg's blinkin' Light Infantry "

Bairnsfather had first hand knowledge of the Intelligence Department. Summoned to the War Office at the end of a period of leave 'amongst the leafy calm of Warwickshire' in 1915, he was informed the he was 'to be placed in the Intelligence Department, to be used, pictorially, for certain work... and initiated into a lot of details dealing with the Intelligence Department!' At one stage they considered asking Bruce to conceal propaganda messages in his replies to the many letters that he received but the idea was dropped.

Nobbled

" 'Ow long are you up for, Bill ?"
"Seven years"
" Yer lucky ——, I'm duration"

Only the small number of professional soldiers of the B.E.F. would have signed on for a specific number of years - often a curious combination of 7's and 3's, e.g. 7 years regular service and then 3 years in the TA. As there was no conscription in Great Britain at the outbreak of War the country depended on volunteers to boost its forces. Kitchener's highly publicised poster campaign was so successful that 100,000 men enrolled in his 'New Army' in the first month. They would have enlisted 'for the duration'. However once the war started it would be unlikely that any soldiers would be released.

Happy Memories of the Zoo
" What time do they Feed the Sea-Lions, Alf ? "

The 'walrus' moustache was well-named as sported by Old Bill. The moustache came to be his trademark and years after the War Bairnsfather had only to scribble the lightning outline of a button nose surmounting the distinctive whiskers for his audience to recognise the much-loved character. This was Bruce's habitual design for fans' autograph books.

63

Observation

''Ave a squint through these 'ere, Bill ; you can see one of the ————'s eatin'
a sausage as clear as anythin' ''

The Germans' fondness for sausage was one of Tommy's most habitual clichés and often expressed in cartoon comment by drawing the Germans as dachsunds (sausage dogs). We sense more than a little envy by Bill and friend, who have obviously dined not too well on the despised tinned rations.

The Communication Trench

PROBLEM—Whether to walk along the top and risk it, or do another mile of this

---

This cartoon probably results from a particular personal experience: 'I entered the communication trench. It was just a deep narrow slot cut across the field and had, I imagine, never been used. I think the enormous amount of water in it had made it a useless work... A fearful trench it was, with a deep deposit of dark, green filthy watery mud from end to end... I plunged into this unwholesome clay ditch and went along, each step taking me up to my thighs in soft dark ooze, whilst here and there the water was so deep as to force me to scoop out holes in the clay at the side when, by leaning against the opposite side with my feet in the holes, I could slowly push my way along'. Using the trench, however, was generally preferable to walking along the parapet and being a target for enemy snipers.

Old Saws and New Meanings——By Bairnsfather

There is certainly a lot of truth in that Napoleonic maxim, "An army moves on its stomach"

Basic training for Kitchener's New Army took place in the UK. Salisbury Plain was a traditional training area and it was there that Capt Bairnsfather was despatched in Spring 1916 to train new men in fieldcraft and the use of machine guns. At the end of the training he commented of his trainees, 'They were ready for anything and would go

through anything. They fully acted up to it, too, in their splendid performance a few months later on the Somme'.
It was while he was at Sutton Veney in 1915 that Bairnsfather drew his most famous cartoon, 'The Better 'Ole'.

67

Letting Himself Down

Having omitted to remove the elastic band prior to descent, Herr Franz von Flopp feels that the trial exhibition of his new parachute is a failure

Though Franz von Flopp's parachute seems somewhat useless, at least he was issued with one. The decision makers in the Royal Flying Corps held the view that 'possession of a parachute might impair a pilot's nerve when in difficulties'. So RFC pilots had to do without them (although balloonists were issued with them) even though by 1917 the German, French and American pilots had them.

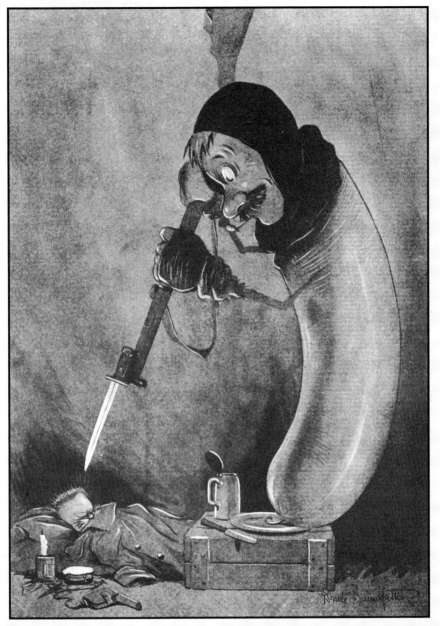

His Dual Obsession

Owing to the frequent recurrence of this dream, Herr Fritz von Lagershifter
has decided to take his friends' advice: Give up sausage late at night and
brood less upon the possible size of the British Army next spring

*However indigestible the sausage was, Fritz would have been considered fortunate to have any at all by his
starving civilian compatriots in Germany. Every effort and sacrifice was made to keep the soldiers well supplied
while, to the civilian, 'ersatz', meaning artificial or substitute, became part of the common language. By 1918
food in Germany was very scarce and civilians were reduced to eating bread containing sawdust and 'roof
rabbits' (rats).*

69

"Where do yer want this put, Sargint?"

Bairnsfather drew this whilst on leave at Bishopton, the family home near Stratford. There he was visited by Vivian Carter, Editor of 'The Bystander', to whom he explained 'It's just a pathetic little whisp of humanity who happens to be, like millions of others, engaged in the entirely unfamiliar business of war… To him, the disposal of that tripod is of more importance than the whole future of Serbia or Belgium. It is the problem of the War.'

Alas! Poor Herr Von Yorick!

Fricourt—July, 1916

On 1 July 1916 the 'Big Push' (Tommy's name for the Somme Offensive) began. Bairnsfather's own regiment, the Royal Warwickshires, was heavily involved in the fighting for the area around Fricourt (although he was not serving with them at the time). Fricourt was taken on 2 July and it seems likely that Bairnsfather drew this while euphoric about the apparent success of the offensive. Later, as the horrific total of casualties became known, his sensitive nature would have prevented him from being so specific about the event his drawing referred to.

"Two minds with but a single thought, two hearts that beat as one"

Telepathy

" Two minds with but a single thought."

This cartoon seems to indicate the situation a couple of seconds before 'Where did that one go to?' Bill and Bert are now so seasoned that they, and the millions of other like them in the trenches, take imminent destruction as part of everyday life. Above the two rifles on the right of the drawing the top of the rum jar is visible. This one did 'reach its destination' – see page 27.

A Castle in the Air

"A few more, Bert, and that there château won't be worth livin' in."

The men got to accept the destruction of beautiful and historical buildings as a matter of little concern other than to offer them a bit of a 'show'. Bairnfather, watching the destruction of Ypres in April 1915, wrote, 'I sat and watched the flames licking round the Cloth Hall. I remember asking a couple of men in front to shift a bit so that I could get a better view.'

The Freedom of the Seas

"I wish they'd 'old this war in England—don't you, Bill?" (No answer)

This comedy situation was used as a scene in the first film to be based on Bairnsfather's cartoons – 'The Better 'Ole', produced by Welsh-Pearson in 1918. Charles Rock played Old Bill, Arthur Cleave, Bert and Hugh E. Wright, Alf. The film was based on the stage play of the same name which Bairnsfather wrote in collaboration with Capt the Hon Arthur Eliot.

Urgent

"Quick, afore this comes down!"

Another illustration of the casual attitude one had to develop towards danger in order to be able to endure it. Sharing out rations was just as vital to Tommy's survival as sheltering from flying debris. Rations would generally be brought up from rear areas under cover of darkness and food that had started out hot often became stone cold by the time the ration party had struggled through all the communication trenches.

75

That tin hat feels something like this on the way to the offensive

And about like this when you get there

My Hat!

Helmets, Shrapnel, One.

Tommy started the war with no protective headgear, whereas the German soldiers had the old fashioned, distinctive, spiked Pickelhaubes. When the 'dish' tin helmet was first issued on trials to the British in 1915, the wearers were fired upon by their own infantrymen, who mistook them for Germans.

"The Imminent, Deadly Breach"

"Mind you don't fall through the seat of yer trousers, 'Arry!"

The quote from 'Othello' indicates that Bairnsfather didn't spend his entire time at school sketching in the margin of his Shakespeare as he often claimed in biographical articles. This illustrates his sublime gift for taking the grandiose concept and applying it to the parochial. 'Arry' is cooking over a fire in a 'flimsy', a thin metal can that was much in used in 1942 for a 'brew up' in the Western Desert.

77

Augusts Three

To each year its type.

Bairnsfather used this idea spread over three separate pages in the 'Toc H Annual' for 1928, to which he and Mabel Lucie Attwell, John Hassall, Rudyard Kipling, A.A. Milne, W. Heath Robinson and many others freely gave their services in order to raise money for the Toc H endowment fund. The Rev Tubby Clayton's Rest House in Poperinghe, Talbot House, can still be visited today and has an interesting museum. The organisation which grew from it is now world-wide, long after Tubby's death. 'Toc H' was the army signallers' phonetic way of spelling out T. H. – for Talbot House.

"Under the spreading chestnut tree the village smithy stands"

Bairnsfather loved the countryside, especially that area of Warwickshire round his home at Bishopton, near Stratford. Before the War, and during the last years in Worcestershire in the 1950s, he painted many fine landscapes though the Royal Academy refused to accept any for exhibition. The devastation of the French and Belgian land and villages made a profoundly sad and lasting impression on him.

His Christmas Goose

"You wait till I comes off dooty!"

The first Christmas of the War was marked by an extraordinary bout of fraternisation between the British and German troops, which was totally unauthorised and heavily frowned upon by the Staff. Bairnsfather was involved in such an episode. 'It was just like the interval between the rounds in a friendly boxing match. After months of vindictive sniping and shelling, this little episode came as an invigorating tonic and a welcome relief to the daily monotony of antagonism'. It is unlikely, however, that Bruce got goose for his Christmas lunch.

Those Signals

THE VIGILANT ONE: "I say, old chap, what does two green lights and one red one mean ?"

RECUMBENT GLADIATOR (just back from leave): "Two crèmes de menthe and a cherry brandy!"

Although radio played an increasingly important part in communication as the war progressed the early sets were very unreliable and several men were needed to carry the batteries. Communication at the front was mostly by runner (Hitler was one), light signal, cable or pigeon. By 1918 there were over 20,000 pigeons serving in the Royal Signals.

"Old Moore" at the Front

"As far as I can make out from this 'ere prophecy-book, Bill, the seventh
year is going to be the worst, and after that every fourteenth!"

Note the aeroplane in the top left hand corer. The first significant contribution made to the war by aeroplanes were the reports sent back by reconnaissance aircraft which spotted von Molke's change of direction when marching towards Paris. Von Moltke did not follow the German invasion plan (known as the Schlieffen Plan) which called for him to keep to the West of Paris. Instead he approached to the East and in so doing may have lost the War. Old Moore's Almanac was initiated by Francis Moore, astrologer in the Court of King Charles II, in 1697. Published annually it predicts world and sporting events.

Supra-Normal

Captain Mills-Bomme's temperature cracks the thermometer on seeing his recent daring exploits described as "On our right there is nothing to report"

(He and his battalion had merely occupied three lines of German trenches, and held them through a storm of heavy Lyddite for forty-eight hours)

Bairnsfather had plenty of experience of military hospitals. After he was wounded at Wieltje near St Julien in April 1915 he was first sent to the military hospital at Boulogne. As his wound was a 'Blighty one' he was then shipped to the 4th London General Hospital where he stayed for several weeks. Later he was again hospitalised at Rouen with a carbuncle on the back of the neck – 'to my mind one of the most degraded forms of heroism'. This was followed by a period of convalescence in a Camberley Military Hospital.

Overheard in an Orchard

Said the Apple to the Plum : "Well, anyway, old man, they can never ask <u>us</u> what we did in the great war!"

Tommy's rations invariably contained plum and apple. Ham and the appearance of any other variety of food was a cause for celebration. Maybe the message of Col Fitz-Shrapnel on page 19 is designed to find out HOW he got raspberry jam. Bairnsfather uses the same theme in a good number of cartoons. Another illustrated here is 'The Eternal Question' on page 44.

The Candid Friend

" Well, yer know, I like the photo of you in your gas mask best "

The Germans were the first to use gas and did so on 22 April 1915 during the Second Battle of Ypres. Bairnsfather was in this battle and in the area in which the gas was released. However the 'Blighty one' that he received on 24 April was due to a shell. At first British troops had to improvise masks from handkerchiefs or the artillery picric acid masks, but miners and firemen had had the protective masks for some time and development was rapid, leading to the Small Box Respirator, which became the British Army's most used mask. A good display of masks can be seen at the Passchendaele Memorial Museum.

The Long and the Short of It

UP LAST DRAFT: "I suppose you 'as to be careful 'ow you looks over the parapet about 'ere"

OUT SINCE MONS: "You needn't worry, me lad; the rats are going to be your only trouble"

Bairnsfather's cartoons amuse by the simplicity of his drawing and also by the captions he added. Yet the captions themselves are rarely simple because, unlike many cartoonists who think of a caption and then illustrate it, Bairnsfather drew the situations which he then had to caption. 'The Innocent Abroad' on page 26 comments on the difference in status and attitude between the soldiers of the B.E.F. and Kitchener's New Army. This cartoon does too, and uses as a foil the rat. Rats in their millions occupied the trenches, living on the dead bodies of men and animals.

Natural History of the War
THE FLANDERS SEA LION (LEO MARITIMUS)
"An almost extinct amphibian, first discovered in Flanders during the Winter of 1914-15. Feeds almost exclusively on Plum and Apple Jam and Rum. Only savage when the latter is knocked off "

Old Bill's resemblance to a walrus or sea lion was recognised even before Bairnsfather drew him in this guise. After the War, performing sea lions in circus and vaudeville acts throughout the world were christened 'Old Bill'.

87

Things that Irritate

Private Wm. Jones is not half so annoyed at accidentally falling down the mine crater as he is at hearing two friends murmuring the first verse of "Don't go down the mine, Daddy."

An original of this drawing is in the Imperial War Museum. We say 'an', rather than 'the' original as Bairnsfather often repeated the same cartoon idea, with small variations, for different publications. 'The Bystander' sold certain of the Post-War 'Fragments' originals in 1919, the proceeds going towards 'relieving of cases of real hardship among ex-soldiers and their dependents'. Following in that tradition this collection of cartoons has been published 90 years later to support the charity Help for Heroes.

Entanglements

"COME ON, BERT, IT'S SAFER IN THE TRENCHES"

At the request of the French Army Intelligence Department, Bairnsfather was sent to the French front line to make sketches in the hope that he could capture the hearts and imaginations of the French people as he had the British. He left England shortly after his appointment as (his words) 'an official and fully licensed humorous cartoonist'. His joining instructions told him which unit to go to but not where it was and en route he spent a night in Paris. At a loss for something to do he went to the Folies Bergère with its 'gaudy, doubtful women' and 'came to the conclusion that there are other dangers besides the trenches'. Hence this drawing. The apologies are to Kirchner because he was the 'glamour' artist par excellence of WW1. His popular, scantily clad young ladies were the originators of the word 'pin-up', as they were, literally, pinned up in the dugouts. Young officers competed with each other to collect the most Kirchner pictures.

The declaration of war by Britain technically committed her Empire to the conflict. There were no reservations by the members, who responded immediately and voluntarily. Canada, New Zealand, Australia and India sent troops to France and other theatres, while South Africa took on the Germans in South-West Africa as well as on the Western Front. Australia also contributed the light cruiser 'Sydney' which had a memorable encounter with the German 'Emden' in November 1914, and the submarine AE2.

The Whip Hand

Private Mulligatawny (the Australian Stock-whip wonder) frequently causes a lot of bother in the enemy's trenches

There are times when Private Lightfoot feels absolutely convinced that it's going to be a War of Exhaustion

The landscape looks typical of the Passchendaele area after the drainage system was destroyed by the constant bombardment in June 1917. The land became a sea of mud, passable only on duckboards such as Private Lightfoot is using. Many men who fell off the duckboards at night were sucked under by the mud and drowned. The 'War of Exhaustion' is an allusion to the phrase 'War of Attrition' which became the policy of both sides during and after the Battle of the Somme in July 1916, i.e. to kill so many of the enemy's soldiers that he is forced to surrender for lack of reinforcements.

91

Real Sympathy

"I wish you'd get something for that —— cough o' yours. That's the second time you've blown the blinkin' candle out!"

No wonder Bert has a cough, for the men in the trenches lived day after day in pouring rain. Clothes and footwear were seldom properly dry. The winter of 1916/17 was exceptionally harsh and mysterious diseases, with the blanket name of 'Trench Fever', swept through the lines. Patent medicines like Sanatogen and Byogen did a roaring trade.

Coming to the Point

"Let's 'ave this pin of yours a minute. I'll soon 'ave these winkles out of 'ere."

Winkles, a favourite delicacy for the working classes (and which one prised from the shell with a special pin) would have been remembered with longing by men on wartime rations. The bayonet was a weapon the soldiers felt they could rely upon and British propagandists encouraged the belief that the Germans 'didn't like cold steel'. The French, in particular, revered the bayonet, which they affectionately called 'Rosalie'. Corporal Jones of 'Dad's Army' used to say, 'They don't like it up 'em, sir'.

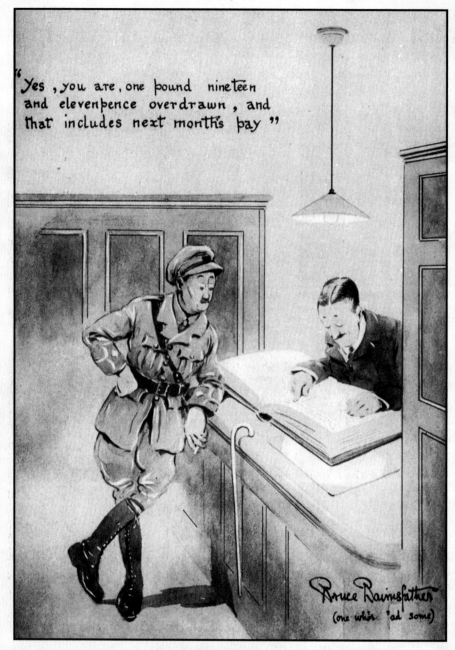

Cox's

When one feels rather in favour of floating a War Loan of one's own

Officers could have their pay handled by the Army Paymaster or by one of two private banks – one advantage of the latter being that sometimes an overdraft could be arranged. Cox's Bank had been established under military patronage in India in 1758 and Bairnsfather had his account there, probably because of his family connections with India. This drawing was done after his formal appointment as an officer cartoonist, when he drew out some cash from Cox's to celebrate.

Unappetising

Moments when the Savoy, the Alhambra, and the Piccadilly Grill seem very far away (the offensive starts in half an hour)

The wistful look on the young officer's face recalls leave-time blow-outs in London restaurants which still managed to provide a decent meal for their clients – especially if in khaki – despite rationing. The last minutes before 'going over the top' were certainly an appropriate time for young officers to reflect on the good things, for the average life expectancy of a subaltern on the Western Front was measured in days.

95

A Miner Success

" They must 'ave 'ad some good news or somethin', Alf; you can 'ear 'em cheerin' quite plain "

Miners were actually brought out to the front from Britain to dig the many miles of tunnels and underground chambers that riddled the French and Belgian ground. It was the Germans, however, who were the underground masters. Their well-made and fortified dugouts afforded them safety from the heaviest bombardment, especially along the famous Hindenburg Line. Nevertheless the most successful British offensive of the war involving mines was probably that at Messines in 1917 when 19 mines were blown around the ridge before the infantry assault. At least one mine of those actually laid has yet to explode and it is probably in the area of la Petite Douve Farm where Bairnsfather was serving in 1914-15. The mine crater at La Boisselle on the Somme, known as Lochnagar, was bought by Englishman Richard Dunning and he now maintains it as a memorial with an annual ceremony on 1 July.

Birds of Ill Omen

" There's evidently goin' to be an offensive around 'ere, Bert "

The ordinary soldier rarely saw Staff Officers in the trenches. Command Headquarters were often in comfortable chateaux – sometimes as much as 8 miles from the front Line – and many stories are told of Staff Officers who sent men into battle without ever having seen the conditions under which they lived and fought.

As Old Bill surmises, a deputation of this strength must mean that 'something was up'. A similar deduction was made when extra rations of rum were made and in WW2 American soldiers, whose army was 'dry', came to the same conclusion when they got steaks to eat.

97

If Only They'd Make "Old Bill" President of Those Tribunals

"Well, what's your job, me lad?"
"Making spots for rocking-horses, sir"
"Three months"
"Exemption, sir?"
"Nao, exemption be ———d! Three months' hard!".

Putting Old Bill in such a responsible position is a foretaste of the second play Bairnsfather wrote about him, 'Old Bill M. P.'. The suggestion that 'Old Bill should go to Parliament' was made to him by Winston Churchill after they had lunched together towards the end of the War. It was not the smash hit that its predecessor, 'The Better 'Ole', was and cost Bruce a great deal of money and headaches.

Alas! My poor Brother!

(In this cartoon Captain Bairnsfather refers to the report that the corpses of German soldiers fallen in battle were utilised in a Corpse-Conversion Factory for the purpose of providing fats for the Fatherland)

The Berlin newspaper 'Lokal-Anzeiger' of 10 April 1917 reported the activities of the Corpse-Conversion Establishment, where bodies were boiled down to produce fat and lubrication. The report did not actually state that human remains were used but referred to animal corpses. However, the allied propaganda machine seized on the story and implied that the corpses of fallen German soldiers were used for this purpose.

That Periscope Sensation

" I wonder *if* I oughtn't to tell the captain about that thing sticking up in the sea over there "

The German U-boats were extremely effective. In April 1917, when the Germans were pursuing a policy of unrestricted submarine warfare, they sank 373 allied ships, the largest monthly total of the War. The most famous (or infamous) U-boat was the U-20, which sank the passenger liner 'Lusitania', with many neutral American passengers on board, on 7 May 1915.

Breweries, with their huge vats which could be filled with steaming hot water to make communal baths, were ideal bath houses. The hot soak was one of Tommy's occasional luxuries, when he could rid himself of lice for a while and be issued with clean clothing. Bairnsfather remembers with affection a visit to the baths in the lunatic asylum in Bailleul. The inmates 'pulled faces' at the soldiers as they arrived and left but inside were 'Soap, sponges, towels ad lib. You can imagine what this palatial water grotto meant to us when, at other times, our best bath was of saucepan capacity, taken on the cold stone floor of a farm room. Glorious!'

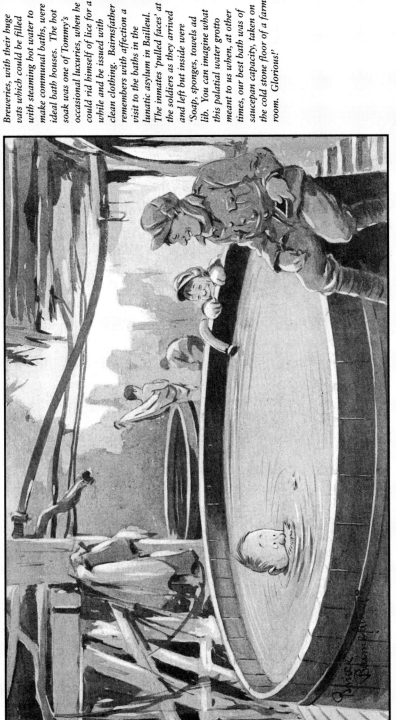

At the Brewery Baths

" You chuck another sardine at me, my lad, and you'll hear from my solicitors "

Romance, 1917

" Darling, every potato that I have is yours " (engaged).

By 1917 food was in extremely short supply. The U-boat campaign was hitting imported foods hard and one in four of the merchant ships leaving British ports was sunk. Staple commodities like eggs, bread and potatoes became very expensive and were frequently the subject of cartoon comment. Their Majesties, King George V and Queen Mary, set examples of frugality by becoming teetotal and planting potatoes at Sandringham. They even had ration cards.

A very personal observation by Bairnsfather who said,' I always felt it was essential to know the absolute facts of all situations depicted from a personal experience point of view. To put it shortly, I felt I could not, say, draw a trench joke unless I had lived in the trenches myself... I found that it was difficult for me to draw them even after I had endured, and left, the trenches.'

Getting the Local Colour

In that rare and elusive period known as "Leave" it is necessary to reconstruct the "Atmosphere" of the front as far as possible in order to produce the weekly "Fragment."

Modern Topography

" Well, you see, here's the church and there's the post-office "

Bairnsfather was a country boy at heart. Before going to school he lived with an Uncle who was the Rector of Thornbury with a Vicarage near Bromyard in Worcestershire. He wrote, 'It was a peaceful ultra-rural existence, which has left me with a complete but slightly melancholic understanding of remote country life ever since.' At the end of his life he lived in another quiet spot in Worcestershire – Littleworth. He felt the destruction of the countryside by the War very badly and the light-heartedness of this drawing conceals a deep personal pain.

A Puzzle for Paderewski

" It's a pity Alf ain't 'ere, Bert ; 'e can play the piana wonderful "

Major Thomas Bairnsfather, Bruce's father, was a very musical man and he produced several musical comedies while serving in India. On his retirement to England he frequently organised musical evenings and Bruce would sometimes join in. Perhaps this was a 'Wish you were here' greeting to his parents, for his letters home were liberally sprinkled with sketches.

The Price of a Pint!

"As far as I can make out from the papers, Bert, breweries seem to 'ave been 'ard
'it by this blinkin' war!"

Bairnsfather had an extraordinary eye for detail which he loved to utilise as often as possible. The obvious place to observe people, particularly once he had left the trenches, was in a bar. Early in the War he was well known at the Wheatsheaf Hotel in Newport, I. O. W., and the Crown Hotel in Warwick. The Queen's Hotel at Farnborough was another favourite haunt and it was here in July 1915 that he learned from a barmaid of his promotion to Captain.

"Old Bill" at Madame Cheerio's

"You are shortly going on a journey across a field ; an ugly man with a square head will cross your path ; you will then hear a loud noise, after which you will rise very high in your profession." (Old Bill, incited by Bert to have his fortune told before returning to the front, didn't like the sound of this forecast at all)

Whatever Old Bill thought of Madame Cheerio's powers, Bruce probably thought better. He disliked the word 'religion' though he frequently pondered on the nature of God, and he described his beliefs as 'a mixture of the sermon on the Mount, Kipling's 'If', Omar Khayam and Astronomy.'

107

The Point of View

"Well, if it don't get merrier than this by Christmas, it won't be up to much"

It did get a bit merrier for Christmas 1914, when an unplanned cessation of hostilities took place on both German and Allied sides and combatants met to exchange souvenirs and rations, to take photographs and play football. Princess Mary's brass tin containing tobacco was also given out to all serving men. From 1915 onwards, however, the Christmas Truce was no longer observed and all available brass was used for munitions.

Duty before Pleasure

"Well, if yer thinks yer ought to, I'll lend yer this bit o' mistletoe o' mine"

Bairnsfather was luckier with the Mademoiselles he was billeted with in Belgium – Suzette, Berthe and Marthe. 'I don't know which I liked the best of these three, they were all so cheery and hospitable. Marthe was the most interesting from the pictorial point of view. She was so gipsy-like to look at: brown-skinned, large dark eyes, exceedingly bright, with a sort of sparkling, wild look about her.'

Second-Lieut. Mabel Smells Powder (No novelty)

"There you are, Bert; I told you we'd 'ave 'em 'ere before we'd finished"

In one respect Bill was correct: Women's Services were formed – the Women's Army Auxiliary Corps in 1917; the W.R.N.S. in 1918 and the W.R.A.F., also in 1918. It was, however, the V.A.D.s and other nursing arms who got nearest the action and the only women officially allowed in the Allied Front Line were the 'Two at Pervyse' – Elsie Knocker and Mairie Chisholme. Bairnsfather drew a cartoon for Elsie (who became the Baroness de T'Serclaes) when he was serving at Coxyde, drawing cartoons for the French, in 1916. 'Smells powder' is a phrase that refers to the smell of gunpowder (not face powder) and means 'facing the enemy'.

This is the fate that Old Bill would have preferred for the Kaiser after the War. The reality was quite different. After his abdication in 1918, he lived out his days in comfort in Holland. Nor would Old Bill have approved of the Kaiser's first words on arriving in Holland, 'Now give me a cup of good English tea'.

Old Bill's War-Aim

To live to see a day like this

111

Charlie Chaplin of course.
Under a similar drawing
Bairnsfather wrote a typical BB
pun, 'A Chaplin to the forces
that would have been welcome'.
Bairnsfather came to know
Charlie quite well after the War.
They met at the Ritz and later
Chaplin was a guest at Bruce's
Tudor Manor at Waldridge near
Aylesbury. His brother Sydney
played 'Old Bill' in the
American film of 'The Better
'Ole' in 1926. The title of the
cartoon is a play on the medical
category 'C3' which meant 'non-
combatant'. If C3s were
fighting, the country would be
down to the 'Last Man'.

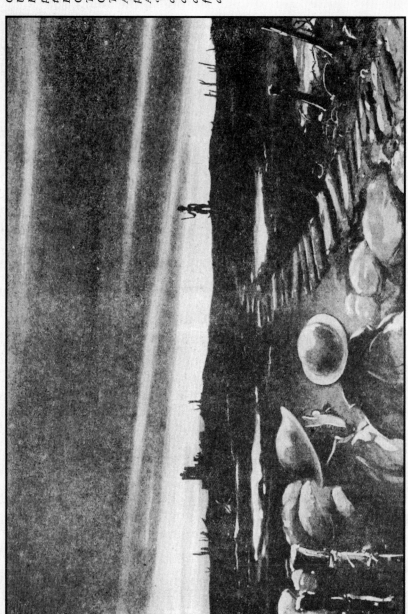

C3. C. C.

THE LAST MAN

112

A Really Welcome Economy

"One shell-less day a week wouldn't be a bad idea, would it, Bert?"

Shells were short on the Western Front in 1916 and the resulting 'Shell Scandal' in June helped bring down the Liberal government – the last ever to hold office. By 1918, although shell supplies were plentiful, there were sometimes two meatless days a week at home in London and in Germany three meatless weeks and more.

Best of *Fragments from France*

Armistice Day, 11 November, or Remembrance Sunday, are the days when we now officially remember veterans and the fallen. The ordeal suffered by millions in the Great War was quickly forgotten by those that did not serve, despite the vows 'We will remember them'. Today it is equally important that we should not forget those who gave their lives, their limbs or their mental health in more recent Wars. Hence 'Help for Heroes'.

19 . . ?

No! This isn't an air-raid bomb bother. Only his grandson Harold, aged eight, has just asked Old Bill what he did in the **great war**

114

Romance Will Return if We Wait Long Enough

"All shell-holes are the same to me when I'm with you, darling"

Many wartime romances sprang up between soldiers, the V.A.D.s and other nursing branches in France and Belgium. One soldier's romance caused a stir when it became public knowledge in December 1975. Then Sotheby's auctioned 99 love letters written by Sir John French to his mistress, Mrs Winifred Bennett. They were said to contain details of troop movements.

A Ticklerish Question

" Funny 'ow we don't seem to get no more plum and apple these days "
" They're usin' it for munitions now, I expect "

The plum and apple jam that so often formed a part of Tommy's rations was made by Tickler's. Rations were always brought forward from the rear in large lots and then split up at regular intervals into smaller lots for distribution. This 'breaking down' of rations was aided by the various packages being marked with the number of men they should feed. Tickler's plum and apple was marked with the unlikely instruction, 'For Three'.

No Joke!

The Censor has been most kind to me throughout the war. I have made the above drawing simply out of gratitude. I have also omitted the joke, thus ensuring complete approval

Bairnsfather was very Censor-conscious because his extraordinary eye for detail meant that his drawings faithfully reproduced what he saw and, sometimes, what others away from the Front were not meant to see. In his wartime books he often inserted remarks like, 'We rattled off down the main street of the village and away to the scene of operations. Where it was I won't say (Cheers from the Censor)'. The notices on the soldiers' faces relate to the criticism by 'The Times' that he portrayed 'a degraded' type of face.

117

His Master's Voice

" What an 'ell of a mess you've made of the name of William "

The Kaiser became the 'Bogeyman' of the Great War as 'Boney' had been during the Napoleonic Wars and Hitler was to become in WW2. He was declared guilty of 'a supreme offence against international morality' in the Peace Treaty of 1919, but the Netherlands, where he was exiled, refused to surrender him and he was never punished. He died in Doorn in June 1941.

The Recruiting Problem Solved

"It strikes me, Bert, if they combed this mud out they might get a
few more men"

---

*Horribly enough, the mud was, of course, full of
bodies – not only of soldiers shot or blown up, but of
soldiers who simply drowned in it. Even today,
farmers along the old Western Front Line dig up
human bones, and after ploughing each year they
collect piles of metal – shells, weapons, equipment etc.*

*They call it the 'Iron Harvest'. Modern archaeological
techniques are discovering even more human remains,
most recently at Fromelles where some 400 British and
Australian bodies were discovered in mass graves in
2008/9. Identification will be attempted from DNA
samples.*

The tank against which Old Bill and co are leaning is in a typical 1916 state – bogged down. The British were the first to use the tank and did so in the Battle of the Somme on 15 September 1916. Haig made the decision to use them in the battle and was later accused of doing so before they were available in large enough quantities to be effective. The popular military expression, still in use today, was that he used them in 'penny packets'.

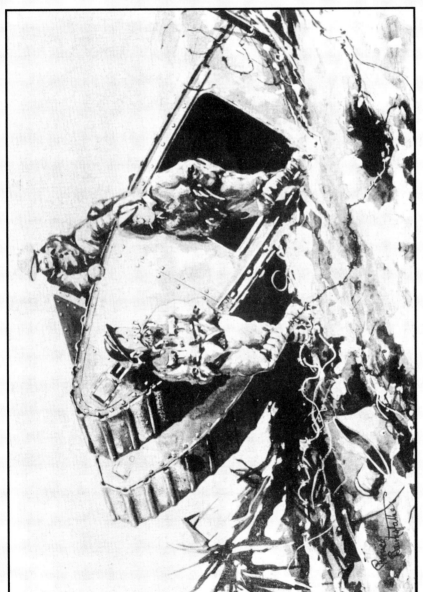

His Fatal Beauty

OLD BILL: "My wife married me for love, ye know, Bert"

BERT: (*after prolonged and somewhat pained scrutiny of Bill's face*): "I had been wonderin' what it was, Bill!"

121

The Raid

"Bert! It's our officer!"

An unusually serious drawing. The genuine grief on Bert and Bill's faces shows the strong bond of love and comradeship that existed between junior officer and soldier. Bairnsfather thoroughly understood this. 'I love those old work-evading, tricky, self-contained slackers – old soldiers! They are the cutest set of old rogues imaginable, yet with it all there is such a humorous, child-like simplicity. They can size up their officers better than any Sherlock Holmes. I'll guarantee that an 'old soldier' will know to a nicety how dirty he can keep his buttons without being hauled up by his new officer after doing one parade under him. If you were lying wounded in the middle of a barrage, that same man would come and pull you out.'

Vindictive, eh?

" I wonder what they'll do with Old Bill when the war's over, Bert?"
" I dunno; 'ave 'im filled with concrete and sunk somewhere, I expect"

Old Bill certainly became a sort of monument after the War. He appeared in the guise of bronze, nickel-plated and brass car mascots, as a china figure, on all manner of pottery items, as a doll, on playing cards, postcards and cigarette cards, in magazines like 'The Bystander', 'Answers', 'The Passing Show', 'The Tatler', 'Illustrated', Time-Life', the 'New Yorker', the 'Royal British Legion Journal'.......and even appeared in films, on the stage and on television.

123

"Ils ne passeront pas"

"Old soldiers never say die, they'll simply block the way"

Bairnsfather's version of Georges Scott's famous painting of the indomitable French Poilu guarding the gateway to France – Verdun. The slogan, 'They will not pass' is attributed to Marshal Pétain. Verdun was to the French Army what Passchendaele was to the British, both in terms of horrendous numbers of soldiers' lives lost and as an emotional symbol of courage and determination.

And a Few Other Things

Napoleon said: "Every soldier carries a field marshal's bâton in his knapsack"

The soldier went into battle carrying an extraordinary range of equipment about his person: a sample mix might be two blankets, groundsheet, spare coat, spare boots, shovel, mess tins, 150 rounds of ammunition, rifle, bayonet, water bottle, towel and many smaller items. The French soldier also carried a couple of litres of wine, hand grenades and gasmasks and while the equipment load of the British was about 65lbs, the Frenchman's was nearer 85lbs and the German's would sometimes exceed even that figure. They all increased vastly in weight when it rained.

125

Perils of War and of Popularity

Old Bill wishes now that he had never gone into that café on the Boulevard des Italiennes

Old Bill's experience looks similar to Bairnsfather's at the Folies Bergères. 'After the usual robbery at the entrance I roamed round the palm court listened to the band, and with the aid of a whisky and soda, watched the fountains squirting water out into the smoke laden atmosphere. What a mass of women they have in that place.' At least two of them played footsie.

127

That Leave Train
"Come on, here's a carriage!"

The identical cartoon appeared in the book, 'C'est Pour la France: Some English Impressions of the French Front' by Capt. A.J. Dawson, illustrated by Capt. Bruce Bairnsfather. Dawson, who was an 'officer descriptive writer' in the same Intelligence Department, and Bairnsfather, collaborated in this way on several book projects, including 'Back to Blighty' and 'Somme Battle Stories'. All were published during the War by Hodder and Stoughton.

A Visit to the Alpini

" The chauffeur says a car fell over here last week "
" Oh ! "

A vivid memory of Bairnsfather's trip to the Dolomite Alps, HQ of the Italian Alpine Regiments. He was driven by the Duke of Milan, whom he found 'an exceptionally nice companion who talked English'. He noted 'An Italian Staff car which was doing its usual ninety miles an hour round impossible corners'. Bairnsfather was requested to do a series of sketches for the Italian armies much as he had been invited by the French. It was his first visit to Italy.

19 . .?

The war was over some time ago, but this man hasn't heard about it yet, and nobody can get up to tell him. His sniping is, therefore, very annoying to that Austrian village in the valley

---

The American artist, Charles Dana Gibson, chose this cartoon as 'the most brilliant thing Bairnsfather ever did in this series'. Gibson, creator of the famous 'Gibson Girl', was President of the Society of Illustrators in the U.S.A. He formed, and became head of, the Division of Pictorial Publicity under the Federal Committee of Public Information. The top American illustrators of the day were used by the Committee to design posters and other publicity for the War effort. After the War Gibson became owner and editor of 'Life' and Bairnsfather did cartoons for this magazine in the Twenties after meeting Gibson in New York. The cartoon reminds one of the Japanese soldiers who, well after WW2 had ended, were reported to pop up from time to time and who were still fighting the War single-handed on some remote Pacific Island.

CAPTAIN BRUCE BAIRNSFATHER
A snapshot taken during one of his visits to the American Army in France

Bruce is pictured with an equine acquaintance here, but he writes, 'I am sorry to say that riding was not, and is not, my forte... I never will be any good at the 'Haute Ecole' *act, I'm sure, although I made several attempts to get a liking for the subject in France... Thank heaven I didn't go into the Cavalry.'*

131

The Two Bills
Both in the same 'ole now !

Bairnsfather revives 'The Better 'Ole' for this, his first published 'Fragment From the American Front'. The American Propaganda Department called for Bruce to 'visit and live with the American Army in the field' just as the first Americans started to come over on 1 April 1917. He toured the American Front in Alsace-Lorraine and soon developed a strong affinity with these 'fine, healthy-looking men'. Once again, in recent Gulf and Afghanistan campaigns, Tommy and Doughboy have been placed in the same 'ole.

America was considered by the Europeans as the Land of Opportunity and Plenty and the Doughboys were regarded as glamorous products of a far-off culture. The fact that they were far better paid than their European Allies added to their attraction to the mademoiselles, much as happened again in WW2. Bairnsfather had this comment about Domrémy, the birthplace of Joan of Arc, 'It's a weird little place, and most gloomy. I don't wish to be disrespectful to the Maid of Orleans, but I feel that if I had been born there myself I should have been bothered with visions too'.

A Land of Dreams

"Ye know Joan of Arc had her visions somewhere around here, Bill"
"I'm not surprised"

Hardly a "Home from Home"

One of those days when you wonder what's going on in Boston, Mass.

Life in Boston, Mass, would have been far removed from life in Alsace-Lorraine. The Home Front in the U.S.A. was not involved in the War in the way that civilians were in Europe (which provided the 'playing field') and, to a lesser extent, in the U.K. Bairnsfather had many connections with Boston after the War during his half a dozen lecture and vaudeville act tours. In 1940 the 'Boston Sunday Globe' ran a series of Bairnsfather's cartoons, starting with an article on him on 28 January entitled, 'How I came to create Old Bill'.

He Soon Found It

" Don't know the way? Wal, keep right on up this track till you
come to a war. Then fight!"

---

*As Bairnsfather soon discovered, 'The American methods are direct and to the point. "Common sense" is
turned on rapidly and clearly'.*

An Eye for Business

WILLIAM K. FLICKER *(the ex-Movie Producer, after surveying the surrounding civilization in silent indignation)* : "Guess they ought to send this outfit on tour when they've finished here!"

A prophetic cartoon, for Bairnsfather gained first-hand knowledge of the American movie producer when 'the Better 'Ole' was made into a film, starring Sydney Chaplin, in 1926. It was produced by Warner Bros. and directed by Charles Reisner. In 1927 the Board of Canadian Films wanted to motivate the Canadian film industry and enlisted Bruce to make a silent film, 'Carry on Sergeant!' Internal arguments, shortage of money, American control of the distribution industry and the advent of talking films all conspired to produce a failure, although today the work is seen as a classic and is available on DVD.

America in France

"I know we're fightin' for Democracy, but next time the Colonel
comes around, salute, you —— son of a — !"

Perhaps the sergeant is referring to an American Colonel, much admired by Bairnsfather and of whom he reported, 'The discipline he maintained was that of a battleship. He called out a few men here and there and ordered certain things to be done to show us details of their routine. Everywhere the whole of his command worked with alacrity and smartness.' Bairnsfather whose military family background had accustomed him to the old order of things, makes another comment about democracy, this time in the British Army, on page 28.

A Small Potato

" What's that hat doin' floatin' round there, sergeant ? "
" I think that's Private Murphy sittin' down, sir "

'My first big impression of America in our European War and an impression I still retain, is: that they seemed to jump in at the point which it had taken us four years to get to. Within a week of landing they looked as if they had been in the War since 1914. They wallowed off into the mud, misery and destruction, without any amateurish deportment.'

Sure Thing

"There's another two million men just arrived from the base sir"
"Well, give them tea, sergeant"

Bairnsfather was highly sympathetic, from personal experience, to the 'daily joys and sorrows' that comprised the RTO's (Regimental Transport Officer) existence. Apart from 'counting rusty truck loads of howitzers or tins of jam; anxiously regarding a prodigious quantity of fifteen-inch shells and wondering when they can be got rid of', he also 'worries over an interminable correspondence which *he finds on many coloured forms (chiefly buff and white) which come floating in to him from all parts of France and from every angle imaginable.' Bairnsfather seems to have got his wires crossed here because the soldiers are American but the officer is giving an instruction known to all those who have ever served in the Army. Presumably an American would say, 'Well, give them coffee, sergeant'.*

139

C'est la Guerre

There were times when I wished Prussian Militarism hadn't forced me to visit America

In 1918 Bairnsfather was sent to America by the Intelligence Department to do propaganda work. He spoke at gatherings to raise funds for Liberty Loans. This is a very personal drawing. He claimed 'the honoured position of the world's worst sailor... Looking at the dock out of the hotel window nearly sends me to bed; there's something about a ship that takes the stuffing out of me completely.' He was to cross the Atlantic nineteen more times between the two World Wars.

" A Sentimental Journey "

I love motoring, but when Silas K. Huckleberry (the accredited war correspondent of the *El Paso Pursuit*) takes me out after a " sob stuff " story, I simply hate it

Who'd Have Thought It?

"'Struth, Bert! Good job we saw that notice!"

What's Bred in the Bone Comes Out in the Bomb

General Sir Francis Drake (a lineal descendant of the great Francis) insists on finishing his game of "bowl bomb" whilst news is brought of an impending attack

The Optimist

" Yer know Bill, with a floor and a roof, a winder and a door or two, you could make quite a nice little 'ome out of this place " (No answer)

19 . . ?

"'Ave ye 'eard any more about them allowin' us
to start 'avin' chevrons on the left arm?"

No Answer

"What's the matter with your 'ead Bill—Pelmanism?
or caught it on a barrage?"

The Dough-Boy in Danger

" Say, you'd better beat it back here; you're standing too close to the war!"

There are several theories for the derivation of the term 'Doughboy', the nickname of the American soldier in WW1. Laurence Stallings, in his definitive history, 'The Doughboys; the Story of the AEF, 1917-1918', writes, 'There can be little dispute as to the derivation of the name. In Texas, U.S. Infantry along the Rio Grande were powdered white with the dust of adobe soil, and hence were called "adobes" by mounted troops. It was a short step to "dobies" and then, by metathesis, the word was Doughboys.'

An In-fringe-ment

"Look 'ere, Bert, if you wants to remain in this 'ere trench be'ave yerself"

Yet another of Bairnsfather's terrible puns, though Bert does look like a young Bill when you add a fringe. In July 1919 Bairnsfather began the production of a weekly magazine called 'Fragments,' for which he was the editor and chief contributor. It was aimed at ex-servicemen and cost twopence. Bairnsfather was contracted for 5 years at the princely sum of £3,000 per annum but the venture lasted only 2 years. The magazine was liberally laced with excruciating puns such as this one.

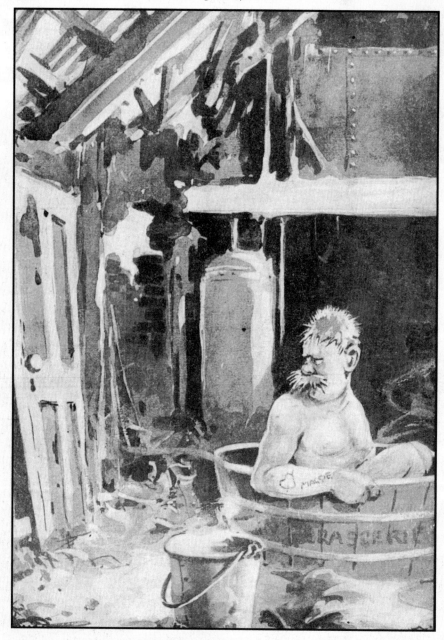

Yet Another 'Ole

"Now then, Bert; none o' yer Lady Godiva squintin' through the key-'ole"

This is not such a luxurious bath as we saw Old Bill taking on page 101, although the receptacle in which he is bathing is still a brewer's vat. Note the tattoo, proclaiming Old Bill's devotion to Maggie, his wife. Tattooing was very popular during the War. In the programme for Bairnsfathr's play, 'The Better 'Ole', at the Oxford Theatre, George Burchett, Tattooist, advertises, 'Crude work covered or removed.' Bairnsfather himself was tattooed.

" 'Ullo ! "

Old Bill celebrates the Armistice by occupying the throne of his namesake, Kaiser Wilhelm. 'Ullo' was Old Bill's catch-phrase, used in future plays and films based on his character. Bruce often drew Bill's head, with this word, in autograph books, on menu cards, and on any other handy scrap of paper, for his admirers. Strangely, what may well be his last published cartoon shows Old Bill saying, 'Cheerio'.

147

Many large buildings such as hotels were requisitioned during the War as hospitals, headquarters etc. The process of demobilisation took many months and compulsory service did not end until 1 April 1920.

Demobilisation

Owing to demobilisation not exactly synchronising with the taking back of the Hotel Terrific by the management, General Sir Claude Cumbersome has to deal with a lot of returns under most impossible conditions

In this drawing Old Bill has reverted to being the civilian he always was under the skin. Bruce often wrote that Old Bill was drawn from the 'working men of Birmingham's vast industrial area', people he 'mixed with and knew to a very intimate degree' before the war. When these Midlands working men joined up it was 'amongst this gathering of reserves and refills for the front line that I subconsciously found the original 'Egg' which hatched into 'Old Bill''.

"Once Upon a Time"

The Wisdom of Bill

"Stick yer 'at pin into Douglas, Maggie. I've known them things go off before now!"

Old Bill as the Bairns' Father

Old Bill's leave (*when he gets it!*) develops into a sort of Baby Week nowadays, since Maggie has left Lome to join the W.A.A.C.'s

---

Battlefield Tours in France and Belgium proved extremely popular for many years after the War with both civilians and veterans. The Royal British Legion ran regular tours until the late 1970s when the compilers, who had recently initiated modern battlefield tours, took over the responsibility until the reinstatement of the Widows' Grant Scheme, when the Pilgrimages were taken back in house. In the 1920s Michelin produced Guides to the Battle Areas. Even Old Bill, like tens of thousands of men, was affected by the increased emancipation of women produced by the war. Maggie has just joined the W.A.A.C.s, who later became Queen Mary's Auxiliary Corps.

The Spirit of "Fragments"

Captain Bairnsfather's Visitation on Christmas Eve

This is a very good rear view of a self-portrait. Old Bill appears as a sort of Marley's Ghost, 'Spirit of Wars past, Present and Future'. He was certainly revived again to serve in the Home Guard in WW2 and a flying Fortress of the 8th USAAF based at Chelveston, Bedfordshire, was named 'Old Bill' and carried Bill's picture on its nosecone, painted by Bruce.

Those Medals

Sad, but true, and apparently unavoidable

It is ironic that the man, who perhaps most of all, deserved the recognition of a national decoration, Captain Bruce Bairnsfather, 'The Man Who Won the War', never received one. After a particularly heavy battle regiments were sometimes given a number of medals to award as they thought fit, so now and again an award was made that was not individually earned. We sponsored a memorial to Bruce on the cottage at St Yvon in Belgium where he drew his first cartoons and initiated a Blue Plaque on his old studio at 1 Sterling Street, Knightsbridge, London.

British K-nights' Entertainments

By a regrettable oversight, the above names were omitted from the last Honours' List

---

There is a touch of unusual vitriol on Bairnsfather's pen here. There was much public indignation over the profits made by some people during the war and 'the Profiteer' was a hated figure (think of Bankers in 2009). In the same way, it seemed to many that civil awards after the War often went to people who had not made any personal contribution to compare to that of the Private soldier. Compare old Bill's reward to that of Pushleigh Grabbe.

153

En Route to a Far, Far Better 'Ole

" 'Struth ! "

Old Bill became Bruce Bairnsfather – or Bruce Bairnsfather became 'Old Bill'. Either way they travelled through post-war life together. They met and worked with the famous: H.G. Wells, Winston Churchill, Edgar Wallace, Houdini, Charlie Chaplin, Sophie Tucker, Sir John Mills ... They wrote a stage play for C.B. Cochran and Darryl Zanuck directed their film for Warner Bros. Their output was prodigious – comic strips, plays, films, books, cartoons, lectures, music hall acts... They toured the world, became official cartoonist's for the U.S.A.A.F. in WW2, appeared on television and tried a space suit. When Bruce died the papers reported, 'Old Bill dies', and they died lonely. This is the story we tell in all its fascinating details in our biography, 'In Search of the Better 'Ole: the Life, the Works and the Collectables of Bruce Bairnsfather', published by Pen and Sword Books.

'TRIBUTE TO BAIRNSFATHER CARTOONS'
DONATED BY SOME OF THE WORLD'S TOP CARTOONISTS

*To be auctioned in aid of HELP FOR HEROES
on 29 September 2009 the 50th Anniversary of Bairnsfather's death.*

Lisa Donnelly,
The New Yorker et al

COIFFURE in the TRENCHES

Philippe Bossens,
Prize-winning
Belgian artist

Well, if you knows of a better pole, go to it

'Matt' (Matthew Pritchett, MBE)
Daily Telegraph Pocket
Cartoonist

" Well, if you knows of a better Olé, go to it "

Kurt Vangheluwe, Belgian
cartoonist, *Talbot Times* et al

'WELL, IF YOU KNOWS OF A BETTER 'OLE, GO TO IT!'

Oliver Preston, Chairman
Cartoon Art Museum, *Field
Magazine, Country Life* et al

Chris Riddell, political cartoonist *The Observer, The Economist* et al

Nicholas Garland,
political cartoonist
The Daily Telegraph

"WELL, IF YOU KNOWS OF A BETTER 'OLE, GO TO IT!"

Steve Bell,
Cartoon Art
Trust Prize winner,
political cartoonist
The Guardian

" Well, if you knows of a better 'ole, go to it."

Michael Cummings, *The Daily Express*,
Punch et al

Well, if you knows of a better 'ole, go to it!

Peter Schrank, *The Independent, New Statesman* et al

157

Jacques Sandron, prolific Belgian
cartoonist of many newspapers
and magazines

Bryn Parry, Co-Founder
Help for Heroes

Martin Rowson, *The Guardian*, *The Daily Mirror* et al

'JACRI' (Christian Jacot) Belgian
comic strip, caricature illustrator,
commercial artist

Herbert Vanoystaeyn, Frequent
prize winner of international
and Belgian contests

Dave Chisholm, *Sunday Times, Mail on Sunday,
Daily Telegraph* et al

Ludo Goderis, Belgian artist for *De Standaard*,
Columbia Pictures, Nestlé et al

OUR SUPPORTERS

Here we say 'Thankyou' to those who have helped with this project

The Belgian Ambassador of H.M.The King of the Belgians, Jean-Michel Veranneman de Watervliet

The Ambassador has been a positive and enthusiastic supporter of our idea from the moment that we mentioned it to him. He immediately offered his London Residence for the launch of the book and agreed without reservation to write the Foreword. Under his tutelage a series of lectures about Belgium and the First and Second World Wars was held during 2008 and will continue in 2009. More details can be obtained from Ann Willems at ann.willems@diplobel.fed.be

Charles Hewitt, Managing Director of Pen and Sword Books and his team

Without a moment's pause Charles agreed to publish the book. His support was clearly essential to the whole idea. We are immensely grateful to him. His company publishes what is probably the most extensive list of military titles available today and fitting in *The Best of Fragments from France* cannot have been a simple commitment. Everyone at Pen and Sword has been wonderfully responsive and tolerant of our often demanding communications, none more so than our designer David Hemingway. www.pen-and-sword.co.uk

Oliver Preston and Anita O'Brian of the Cartoon Museum

Over the last few years we have loaned a series of original Bairnsfather cartoons to the Cartoon Museum whose Curator is Anita. She has always given us a warm welcome despite a heavy work load with a series of exhibitions and when we mentioned the idea of an auction she agreed straight away. Chairman Ollie Preston offered the Museum gratis and volunteered to approach the cartoonists for their drawings and to initiate the invitations to the Auction. http://www.cartoonmuseum.org

The Cartoonists

Without the generous support of the cartoonists there would not be an auction and without the auction the monies raised for Help for Heroes would be greatly reduced. Each contributor has made a very special gesture of donating a piece of their art that links our soldiers over almost 100 years and pays homage to one of their own greats - Bruce Bairnsfather. It is particularly pleasing that not only do we have cartoons from some of the UK's top cartoonists but drawings from America and Belgium as well. We had been looking for 20 cartoons, the majority of which appear in *The Best of Fragments From France*. That number will be slightly exceeded at the auction and some of the great Belgian cartoons that we have received will be shown in a special Exhibition at Comines-Warneton in October. 2009.

Michel van Pottelberghe, Bibliothécaire-secretaire Société d'Histoire de Comines-Warneton

We first met Michel in 2003 when we put up the memorial to Bruce Bairnsfather on the cottage at St Yvon. He and the Burgomaster Albert Deleu dealt with all the details of the ceremony and arranged the vin d'honneur and celebrations that followed. Once more they have helped with this 50th Anniversary Project and now have a specified local tour around the points of Bairnsfather interest in the area of 'Plugstreet Wood'. www.shcwr.org

Joe Bristow, Bairnsfather enthusiast and Contributor to the Auction.

Joe has amassed a formidable collection of Bairnsfather cartoons and collectables, much of which is shown on his fascinating tribute website www.brucebairnsfather.com. Joe was the first visitor to this site who volunteered to donate a cartoon and a Bairnsfather original at that. Thankyou Joe, that gift truly is a magnificent gesture.

Jan Oplinus, ECC Cartoonbooks Club

Jan has always had a passion for books about cartoons and, there not being a club for fellow enthusiasts, started the European Cartoonbooks Club in collaboration with the European Cartoon Center based in Kruishoutem, Belgium. Members, from around the world, own some 20,000 cartoon books. Jan only recently 'discovered' Bairnsfather, who served in the WW1 trenches only 26kms from his home. He has become a great enthusiast for the BB4H4H project - spreading the news among cartoonists and members worldwide. Several of them have donated BB-inspired cartoons as a result of his efforts and their work will be exhibited in Comines-Warneton in October 2009. ecc.cartoonbooks@gmail.com www.ecc-cartoonbooksclub.blogspot.com

James Knight, Bonhams Auctioneers

James has specialised in motoring auctions for 25 years and those who have attended one of his sessions will know of his great sense of humour and his ability to entertain his audience while at the same time obtaining the best prices for the vendors. Nominated for the British Antiques and Collectors Association 'Auctioneer of the Year' award, James' most spectacular lot was that of the world's oldest Rolls Royce which sold for over £3.5m. When we asked James to conduct the cartoon auction he agreed without hesitation. Thankyou James. james.knight@bonhams.com

Mark Warby, Editor *The Old Bill Newsletter*

We have known Mark for many years. At first he was just a young enthusiast eager to learn more about Bruce Bairnsfather but a more assiduous searcher after facts and memorabilia would be hard to find and today he edits *The Old Bill Newsletter*, which six times a year astounds its subscribers with new information about Bruce Bairnsfather and his works. Mark has travelled from Australia to America, to Belgium and to France in pursuit of his passion and all collectors owe him a great debt. Nothing escapes his eagle eyes from offerings on the internet to the more remote of local auctions. No self-respecting collector of Bairnsfatherware should be without Mark's magazine. www.brucebairnsfather.org.uk

Western Front Association

Bruce Simpson , WFA Chairman, became a friend of ours when he came on one of our battlefield tours as a boy with his father. He has wholeheartedly supported our bb4h project, as has Jon Cooksey, knowledgeable editor of *Stand To* and *The Bulletin*. WFA was formed in 1980 to further interest in the period 1914-1918 and now has branches throughout this country and overseas run and enjoyed by enthusiastic and committed members. Their purpose is to perpetuate the memory, courage and comradeship of those of all sides who served their countries during the Great War. www.westernfrontassociation.com

Jane Newton, The British Cartoon Archive

In 1994 we loaned our original copy of Bairnsfather's *Better 'Ole* cartoon for a small exhibition at the University of Kent's British Cartoon Archive and met Jane Newton and Dr Nick Hiley the Head of the Archive. In 1999 the cartoon again arrived at Canterbury as part of the 'A Century of Cartoons Exhibition' sponsored by British Airways. It had started life at the V and A. We rang Jane early in 2009 after a gap of some 10 years and outlined our project. As before she expressed great enthusiasm and helped Anita O'Brian to choose the Nicholas Garland cartoon that is being auctioned and also contacted Dave Chisholm who drew the very current interpretation of something that had haunted Bairnsfather from the day that he was blown up by a shell in April 1915. www.cartoons.ac.uk

Help for Heroes

When we approached Help for Heroes with our idea we were met with extraordinary enthusiasm by everyone that we spoke to despite the overwhelming load of work that they all carry. Mark Elliott was our first contact and his response gave us the impetus to 'go for it'. Bryn Parry found a moment to draw his cartoon as well as listening to our thoughts and Holly Dyer responded to requests for help at such speed that we hardly had time to tell her what we needed. www.helpforheroes.org.uk

So Many Others ...

So many other people have helped us with this project by offering to link the bb4h4h website and the book with their own work. We thank them wholeheartedly and we thank the journalists and magazine editors like Sarah Sturt of *Kent Life*, www.kent-life.co.uk George Harwood, Editor of The Friends of Lochnagar Journal, *The New Chequers*, www.friendsoflochnagar.co.uk and Brian Lund of the *Postcard Collectors Gazette*, www.postcardcollecting.co.uk who have taken an interest in the Anniversary itself as well as in the H4H connection, and have published articles.

And Finally, Nicholas Pine

Nicholas Pine, then of Milestone Publications, who had the confidence and initiative to publish both the original *Best of Fragments* and *In Search of the Better 'Ole* and who has remained a firm friend and supporter.